POJO'S UNOFFICIAL
Ultimate
POKÉMON
TRAINER'S
HANDBOOK

TRIUMPH
BOOKS

Angel Pelaez

Tord Reklev

Matthew Buck

Jason Klaczynski, 2013

Bill Gill, a.k.a "Pojo", 2005

Amy & Anna Gill, 1999

This book is available in quantity at special discounts for your group or organization. For further information, contact:

Triumph Books LLC, 814 North Franklin Street, Chicago, Illinois 60610
Phone: (312) 337-0747
www.triumphbooks.com

Printed in U.S.A.
ISBN: 978-1-63727-317-3

Editor in Chief: Bill Gill, a.k.a "Pojo"
Creative Director & Graphic Designer: Phil Deppen
Writers: Bill Gill, Angel Pelaez, Jason Klaczynski, Tord Reklev, Matthew Buck
Proofreader: Amy Gill
Cover design: Preston Pisellini

From Pojo

25+ Years of Pokémon!

Holy Miltank! Can you believe that Pokémon has been around for over 25 years now?! Pokémon went from a tiny "Little 8-bit Game Boy game that could" into a full-blown ~~juggernaut~~ ... er Melmetal!

The original Red/Blue Pokémon games from 1996 sold over 30 million copies, and Pokémon Sword/Shield games from 2019 has sold over 25 million copies. Pokémon shows no sign of slowing down.

The Pokémon Trading Card Game was also first released in 1996, and is still immensely popular today. There were four new set releases in 2022, bringing the total of Pokémon TCG sets to 100! Plus, the new set for 2023 – Crown Zenith was just releasing about the time we wrote this book.

Also, the anime is still going strong. Ash Ketchum's 25-year story arc comes to a close in 2023. Will Ash retire? We don't know yet, but the Pokémon anime will be focusing on new heroes in a new Pokémon realm. There are big changes in store for fans of the anime.

And we are still busy here at Pojo. We started a website in 1998, wrote our first Pokémon magazine in 1999, and delivered a total of 20 magazines to dedicated fans. Now you are holding our sixth Pokémon Book. I may be turning into an old man, but I still have Pokémon running through my veins.

We tried to give our readers a whole lot of information in this issue. We have a timeline to help you look back on 25+ years of Pokémon. Angel Pelaez has updated the rankings of the video game Pokémon for you to account for the new Scarlet and Violet Pokémon. Matthew Buck gives you an update on the world of Pokémon Go in case you have given that adventure a little break. We also have a 3-time World Champ, and a 4-time International Champ (Jason Klaczynski and Tord Reklev respectively) teaching you what makes good Pokémon cards great in a skilled player's hands.

And that's not all. There are a lot more goodies inside including puzzles, anime reviews, rare finds, and a whole lot more. I hope you enjoy everyone's efforts. The writers, the graphic designers, the proofreaders and the editors poured a whole lot of sweat into making this a great read for you.

Pojo

Our first BIG BOOK!

Our first magazine from 1999!

CONTENTS

POKÉMON TIMELINE

6   A look back at 26+ years of Pokémon releases

POKÉMON ANIME SERIES

20   Ash Ketchum's 25-year journey to World Champion

POKÉMON TRADING CARD GAME

36   The Top 10 cards from every era ranked

58   All about graded Pokémon cards

POKÉMON GO

62   The latest tips and tricks for Pokémon Go

POKÉMON VIDEO GAMES

70   The Top 10 Pokémon by Type

90   Were Pokémon Colosseum and Gale of Darkness ahead of their time?

94   Pokémon Scarlet and Violet reviews

98   The Top 10 Pokémon Role Playing Games Ranked

108   The Pojodex! Pojo's Pokémon Pokédex for Generations I through IX

RARE FINDS

118   A look at some unique Pokémon collectibles

POKÉMON PUZZLES

124   Pojo's Pokémon Puzzlers

The Pokémon Tim_li...

1996 to 2023

By Bill Gill

Pokémon has been around for over 25 years, and is still a worldwide phenomenon. Pokémon has given us: over 100 video games; 25 seasons of anime; an amazing Trading Card Game with nearly 100 expansions; and one of the most-popular mobile games of all-time.

We thought it would be fun to look back at the key products that The Pokémon Company has released over the years. We are breaking out the Wayback Machine and having a stroll down memory lane. We are going to start off by looking at a few major Japanese releases, and then focus soley on American releases.

1996

Pocket Monsters Red & Green in Japan

In February 1996, the Pocket Monsters Red & Green video games were released in Japan. These games introduced the concept of collecting, trading and battling with Pocket Monsters. These two games eventually sold more than 10 million copies in Japan.

Pokémon Trading Card Game (TCG) debuts in Japan

Trading Card Games were a relatively new phenomenon in 1996. Magic: the Gathering debuted in 1993 and had a cult following, but not too many people in the world really knew about TCGs. The Pocket Monsters TCG changed that. The Pocket Monsters TCG became a craze in Japan that was destined to take the world by storm.

The Japanese "Pocket Monsters" franchise name was changed to "Pokémon" in the United States due to copyright/trademark laws. There was already a media franchise in the U.S. named "Monsters in My Pocket". The TCG is still going strong 26 years later.

1997

Pokémon Anime debuts in Japan

Season 1 – The Pokémon Anime has become one most successful anime of all time. As of the writing of this book, there have been over 1,200 episodes of Pokémon! The series follows the adventures of Satoshi and his Pocket Monsters. In North America, Satoshi is called Ash Ketchum, and Pocket Monsters are called Pokémon.

1998

Pocket Monsters Movie – Mewtwo Strikes Back released in Japan

This was the first theatrical release in the Pokémon franchise, and it was a box office success. The film grossed over $172 million at the worldwide box office. The movie also sold over 10 million copies (VHS and DVD) in the United States.

Pokémon Red and Pokémon Blue

The Pokémon Red and Blue Role–Playing Games (RPGs) were released in North America. These were essentially the English remakes of the Pocket Monsters Red and Green video games. These games sold more than 31 million copies worldwide. New, factory–sealed, unopened boxes of these games can sell for over $8000 on eBay.

1999

TRADING CARD GAME

Pokémon TCG debuts in North America with the "Base Set"

When the Pokémon Trading Card Game was released in North America, it took the U.S. by storm! The first set was called the "Base Set". There have been over 100 expansions since the original Base Set.

Jungle – The 2nd Pokémon TCG expansion.

Pokémon Fossil – The 3rd Pokémon TCG expansion.

VIDEO GAMES

Pokémon Yellow – This game was inspired by the anime. This is an updated version of the original Red & Blue games with some fun changes. Pikachu is your starting Pokémon. Pikachu follows you around on your adventure outside of his Poké Ball just like in the anime.

Super Smash Bros. (N64) – One of the best fighting games all of all time. The game features Pikachu and Jigglypuff as playable characters.

Pokémon Pinball (Game Boy Color) – One of the first games available for the new Game Boy Color at the time.

Pokémon Snap (N64) – The player rides through various Pokémon environments in a cart on a track, and takes photographs of Pokémon for Professor Oak. This game is fun and addictive.

ANIME

Season 2 – Adventures on the Orange Islands, 36 episodes – Professor Oak sends Ash to Valencia Island to help Professor Ivy. Ash meets and travels with Tracey Sketchit.

Pokémon the First Movie – The First Pokemon Movie is released in the United States, and debuts at #1 at the box office.

2000

TRADING CARD GAME

Base Set 2 – This set had no new cards. Wizards of the Coast created this set to make older cards easier to collect.

Team Rocket – This is the first set to include Dark Pokémon, with Dark Raichu as the first–ever secret card.

Gym Heroes – The set introduced Gym Leaders and Stadium cards.

Gym Challenge – The second part of the Gym TCG Sets.

Neo Genesis – Features Pokémon from the Johto region for the first time. This expansion introduced Baby, Dark, and Metal Pokémon.

VIDEO GAMES

Pokémon Gold & Silver (Game Boy Color) – Players visit the Johto region for the first time. A total of 100 new Pokémon were added, and Dark and Steel type Pokémon are introduced.

Pokémon Stadium (N64) – Pokémon are in 3D for the first time. This was a battling game, not an RPG. Your favorite Red & Blue Pokémon could be transferred in for battles.

Pokémon Trading Card Game – (Game Boy Color) – This is a video game adaption of the Pokémon TCG. It was an excellent adaption of the TCG at the time.

Pokémon Puzzle League (N64) – This was a Tetris style game with a Pokémon theme.

Hey You, Pikachu! (N64) – A Pokémon Video Game for little kids.

Pokémon Puzzle Challenge (Game Boy Color) – Another Pokémon Puzzler.

ANIME

Pokémon the Movie 2000 – This second Pokémon film made over $130 million dollars at the box office.

Season 3 – The Johto Journeys, 41 episodes – Ash and the gang visit the Johto region and discover new Pokémon from the Gold & Silver video games.

2001

TRADING CARD GAME

Neo Discovery – Tyrogue and Unown C are the stars here.

Neo Revelation – Shining Pokémon make their debut.

VIDEO GAMES

Pokémon Stadium 2 (N64) – This game is essentially a re–release of Pokémon Stadium, except now you can input your Gold & Silver Pokémon using the Transfer Pak.

Pokémon Crystal – Pokémon Crystal is a follow–up, sister–type game to the extremely successful Gold & Silver Games with some minor enhancements. For the first time in a Pokémon game, you can play as a female character!

Super Smash Bros. Melee – This was the first game on the GameCube system to feature Pokémon, and folks loved this game! Mewtwo and Pichu were added as playable Pokémon.

ANIME

Pokémon 3: The Movie – Spell of Unown –This film made over $68 million at the box office.

Season 4 – Johto League Champions, 52 episodes – Ash continues his adventures in the Johto Region with Misty and Brock.

2002

TRADING CARD GAME

Neo Destiny – Dark Pokémon return to the TCG

Legendary Collection – The 2nd reprint set. Includes strong cards from Base Set, Jungle, Fossil and Team Rocket.

Expedition Base Set – The set began the e–Card series where cards had a dot code that the Nintendo e–Reader could scan for lore, minigames, and the like. Packs went down to nine cards, and Holo–rares could replace a common and not the normal rare.

ANIME

Season 5 – Pokémon: Master Quest, 65 episodes – Ash heads to the Whirl Islands and enters the Whirlpool cup.

Pokémon 4Ever – Celebi: Voice of the Forest – This fourth Pokémon movie is the last to receive a theatrical release in the United States.

2003

TRADING CARD GAME

Aquapolis – Crystal Pokémon make their debut.

Skyridge – This was the final set released by Wizards of the Coast as Nintendo took back their license. Cards from this set are extremely collectible.

EX Ruby & Sapphire – This was the first set released by Nintendo, Not WOTC. The set introduced Generation III Pokémon into the TCG. This set introduces EX Pokémon into the TCG for the first time.

EX Sandstorm – This set brought in some nice EX cards.

EX Dragon – This set brought us some Dragon type Pokémon for the first time.

VIDEO GAMES

Pokémon Ruby and Pokémon Sapphire (Game Boy Advance – GBA) – These games introduced over 135 new Pokémon from the Hoenn region (Generation III).

Ruby and Sapphire (GBA) – This is a sequel to Pokémon Pinball for the Game Boy Color. A very underrated Pokémon game.

ANIME

Pokémon Heroes: Latios and Latias – This is the 5th Pokémon Movie. This movie focuses on Ash, Misty and Brock traveling to Alto Mare, a city like Venice, Italy.

Season 6 – Pokémon Advanced, 40 episodes – Ash and friends head into the Hoenn region for the first time. Ash gains new companions in May, a new Pokémon trainer who is just beginning her journey, and her brother, Max.

2004

TRADING CARD GAME

EX Team Magma vs Team Aqua – The first expansion to feature dual–type Pokémon.

EX Hidden Legends – Gave us strong cards like Ancient Technical Machine (Rock) and Steven's Advice.

EX FireRed & LeafGreen – A set of cards based on the Game Boy Advance remakes of the first Pokémon Games.

EX Team Rocket Returns – The first TCG expansion to feature Pokémon Star.

VIDEO GAMES

Pokémon Colosseum (GameCube) – Pokémon Colosseum is essentially an upgrade of the Pokémon Stadium Games for Generation III Pokémon. Unlike the previous Stadium games, this game features a story mode.

Pokémon Box (GameCube) – This was an organizer for the Pokémon you had caught while playing Ruby & Sapphire. This was targeted at diehard Pokémon Fans, and extremely rare. Complete copies of this can sell for $5,000 on eBay!

Pokémon FireRed and Pokémon LeafGreen (Game Boy Advance) – Remakes of the original Red and Blue games, with facelifts to take advantage of the new GBA technology.

ANIME

Pokémon: Jirachi Wish Maker – The sixth Pokémon movie debuts on DVD. The movie features Ash, Brock, Max and May.

Season 7 – Pokémon: Advanced Challenge, 52 episodes – Ash and the gang continue their journey through the Hoenn region.

2005

TRADING CARD GAME

EX Deoxys – The set brought us Jirachi (Wishing Star), which had a huge impact on competitive decks.

EX Emerald – A set released to promote the new Emerald game on the Game Boy Advance. This set featured special holographic basic Energy cards often known as "Matrix Energy" due to their design.

EX Unseen Forces – Unown make their return!

EX Delta Species – This set introduced Delta Species Pokémon, plus Holon's Pokémon that could be used as Energy cards.

VIDEO GAMES

Pokémon Emerald (Game Boy Advance) – This is a follow–up / sister–game to the Ruby and Sapphire Game Boy Advance games, with a few enhancements.

Pokémon XD: Gale of Darkness (GameCube) – This is direct follow up to Pokémon Colosseum. Gale of Darkness has a longer single player campaign than Colosseum, and allows the player to capture some wild Pokémon and transfer them to their handheld games.

Pokémon Dash (DS) – The first Pokémon game for the Nintendo DS (Dual Screen). You control Pikachu in a racing game.

ANIME

Destiny Deoxys – The seventh Pokémon movie premieres on Kids' WB. Ash is accompanied by May, Max and Brock again.

Season 8 – Pokémon: Advanced Battle, 54 episodes – Ash finally earns the last two badges needed to qualify for the Hoenn League Championship. May's final Hoenn Contest also comes around.

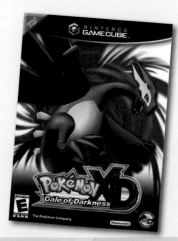

2006

TRADING CARD GAME

EX Legend Maker – React Energy debuts here.

Holon Phantoms – This was first set to bring us δ Delta Species Pokémon.

Crystal Guardians – Delta Species Pokémon–EX make their debut.

EX Dragon Frontiers – Two new mechanics are introduced with this set: Imprison Markers and Shock–wave markers.

VIDEO GAMES

Pokémon Mystery Dungeon: Blue Rescue Team/ Red Rescue Team – These are essentially the same games for different gaming systems. Blue is for the DS, and Red is for the GBA. You are a human who has been turned into a Pokémon, and thrown into a crazy Pokémon World fraught with disasters.

Pokémon Ranger (DS) – Pokémon Ranger introduced a new way to catch Pokémon. You tame and capture Pokémon by drawing circles around them on the Touch Screen.

Pokémon Trozei (DS) – A Pokémon Puzzler that isn't half bad.

ANIME

Pokémon: Lucario and the Mystery of Mew – This is the 8th Pokémon Movie. Ash and gang work with Lucario and Mew to find and save Pikachu.

Season 9 – Pokémon: Battle Frontier, 47 episodes – Ash begins his adventures in the Battle Frontier. May, Max, Brock and Ash journey together.

2007

TRADING CARD GAME

EX Power Keepers – This was the final EX set released. This was the first time since Team Rocket that some cards were designed outside of Japan.

Diamond & Pearl – This set includes Pokémon from the Sinnoh region (Generation IV) for the first time.

D&P Mysterious Treasures – This set gave us the Gen IV Pokémon which Evolved from Fossil cards.

D&P Secret Wonders – Secret Wonders birthed a potent deck with Gardevoir and Gallade.

VIDEO GAMES

Pokémon Diamond and Pokémon Pearl (DS) – Pokémon D&P brought players into the Sinnoh region and introduced over 100 new Pokémon (Generation IV)

Battle Revolution (Wii) – Pokémon Battle Revolution is essentially an upgrade of the old Pokémon Stadium Games with Generation IV Pokémon.

ANIME

Pokémon Ranger and the Temple of the Sea – The 9th film features a new English Voice Cast as 4Kids Entertainment was no longer involved with the Pokémon Anime. This is the last film to feature May and Max as main characters in the series.

Season 10 – Pokémon: Diamond and Pearl, 52 episodes – Ash and Pikachu visit the Sinnoh for the first time. Ash meets and travels with Dawn – a Pokémon Trainer learning to become a Pokémon Coordinator.

2008

TRADING CARD GAME

Diamond & Pearl Great Encounters – The set was created to fill a gap. This set lined up TCG set releases to coincide better with Japan's release dates.

D&P Majestic Dawn – This set brought us the power cards: Unown Q, Call Energy, Empoleon and Scizor.

D&P Legends Awakened – Shortly after this set released, the Standard Format shifted to Diamond & Pearl and later sets (DP–On). The format was worldwide, so even Japan followed it.

D&P Stormfront – Stormfront introduced Shiny Pokémon to the Diamond & Pearl Series.

VIDEO GAMES

Super Smash Bros. Brawl (Wii) – This is the third installment of the Smash Bros. fighting series. The playable Pokémon include: Pikachu, Jigglypuff, Pokémon Trainer and Lucario. This Wii version allowed for 4 players to play local co–op. You could also battle online for the first time.

Pokémon Mystery Dungeon Explorers of Darkness / Explorers of Time (DS) – This is the 2nd installment of Nintendo's Pokémon Dungeon Crawler.

My Pokémon Ranch (Wii) – This was a WiiWare game. You were a "Wii Mii" rancher running a Pokémon Ranch.

ANIME

The Rise of Darkrai – This is the 10th Pokémon movie, and is the first part in a trilogy of Diamond and Pearl films. Ash, Brock, Dawn, and Pikachu visit the town of Alamos.

Season 11 – Pokémon: DP Battle Dimension, 52 episodes – Ash and Brock continue their journey through the Sinnoh region. Dawn tags along again, facing many challenges as a Pokémon Coordinator. Team Galactic is introduced as the new evildoers.

Pokémon Ranger: Shadows of Almia (DS) – This action–adventure game is a sequel to Pokémon Ranger. The game features Pokémon from Generation I–IV.

2009

TRADING CARD GAME

Platinum – This expansion introduced Pokémon SP and the Lost Zone.

Rising Rivals – Pokémon SP could now be Pokémon GL or Pokémon E4. "GL" stood for Gym Leader while "E4" stood for Elite Four.

Supreme Victors – This set brought us two more kinds of Pokémon SP – Pokémon C and Pokémon FB. The "C" was for Champion while "FB" was for Frontier Brain.

Arceus – Each Arceus in this set had a rule printed on it stating you could have as many cards with the name "Arceus" in your deck as you wished. The 60–card deck count still applied.

VIDEO GAMES

Pokémon Platinum (DS) – Pokémon Platinum was a follow–up, sister–type game to the Pearl and Diamond games, with a few changes. The most notable changes were: 59 more Pokémon, more Legendary Pokémon available to capture, a new Distortion World, and a new Villa for your valuables.

Pokémon Mystery Dungeon: Explorers of Sky (DS) – This was a sister game to the Explorer of Time / Explorers of Darkness games. A similar game, but with some nice enhancements.

Pokémon Rumble (Wii) – This was a new type of Pokémon Game. This is strictly an action game. You start off as a low–level Pokémon and battle other Pokémon. Gameplay is essentially real–time melee, smash your opponent type battles. This game supports up to four players simultaneously.

ANIME

Pokémon: Giratina and the Sky Warrior – The 11th Pokémon movie is the second of the Diamond & Pearl trilogy of films. Ash and friends are trying to help the Pokémon Shaymin return to its friends.

Season 12 – Pokémon: Diamond & Pearl Galactic Battles, 53 episodes – Ash, Dawn, Brock and Max continue their journey through the Sinnoh region.

2010

TRADING CARD GAME

HeartGold & SoulSilver – This set introduced Pokémon LEGEND cards and focused on Generation I and II Pokémon.

HS Unleashed – This set introduced Pokémon Prime cards.

HS Undaunted – This set brought more Pokémon Prime and Pokémon LEGEND. Pokémon Prime became a major force in tournaments.

HS Triumphant – The final set in the HS series and the last with Pokémon Prime and Pokémon LEGEND.

VIDEO GAMES

Pokémon HeartGold and Pokémon SoulSilver (DS) – These games were modernized remakes of Gold & Silver. A "Pokéwalker" pedometer was bundled with these games. Players could transfer Pokémon from the game into the Pokéwalker device and walk around with the Pokémon. This would earn the gamer "watts", which could be exchanged for in-game rewards.

Pokémon Ranger: Guardian Signs (DS) – This action-adventure game is a sequel to Pokémon Ranger: Shadows of Almia. It is the best Ranger game in the series.

PokéPark Wii: Pikachu's Adventure (Wii) – This is a single player action-adventure game for children. Cute but very simple game.

ANIME

Arceus and the Jewel of Life – This the 12th Pokémon movie, and it completes the Diamond and Pearl trilogy of films. Ash must help save the World, the Reverse World, Space and Time.

Season 13 – Diamond and Pearl: Sinnoh League Victors, 34 episodes – Ash and Dawn focus on their goals of qualifying for the Sinnoh League Championship and the Grand Festival. Brock considers becoming a Pokémon Doctor.

2011

TRADING CARD GAME

Call of Legends – This expansion included the Lost World Stadium card, which provided a new way to win the game.

Black & White – This first expansion of the Black & White Series was comprised entirely of newly discovered Pokémon from the Unova region.

B&W Emerging Powers – Contains 26 new Pokémon from the Unova region.

B&W Noble Victories – This set brought us the Support Card N, which would become a staple in decks.

VIDEO GAMES

Pokémon Black Version and Pokémon White (DS) – Black and White brought players into the Unova region and introduced over 135 new Pokémon (Generation V). These versions introduce Team Plasma, Seasons of the year, Triple Battles and Rotation Battles.

The Pokémon Trading Card Game Online – The Pokémon TCG Online lasted 10 years and was retired in November 2021. It was a "Free to Download – Free to Play" version of the paper TCG. The game was replaced by Pokémon Trading Card Game Live.

Pokémon Rumble Blast (3DS) – This was the first Pokémon game for the 3DS. This was a sequel to the Pokémon Rumble. This is a simple, cute, fun, and action-packed dungeon crawler.

ANIME

Zoroark: Master of Illusions – The 13th Pokémon movie. Ash, Dawn and Brock travel to Crown City to watch the Pokémon Baccer World Cup. As usual, strange things happen during their visit.

Season 14 – Pokémon: Black & White, 48 episodes – Ash begins a new quest in the Unova region. Ash meets and travels with new friends Iris and Cilan, who are Pokémon Trainers as well. Ash also befriends Trip, a Pokémon photographer, and Bianca, another trainer. Team Rocket returns.

White–Victini and Zekrom & Black–Victini and Reshiram – These two films (14 & 15) are almost identical. Different Pokémon appear in the different versions. Ash and his friends Iris and Cilan have made their way to Eindoak Town, where strange things happen and Ash must save the day.

2012

TRADING CARD GAME

B&W Next Destinies – The first set to officially introduce the powerful Pokémon–EX into the game. Not only were Pokémon bigger than before, but they were more powerful too.

B&W Dark Explorers – This set provided a bunch of powerful cards for Dark decks, with Darkrai–EX leading the way.

B&W Dragons Exalted – This set officially introduced Dragon–type Pokémon to the TCG.

B&W Boundaries Crossed – The ACE SPEC game mechanic was introduced here. This allowed for very powerful cards to be printed, but they were limited to one card per deck.

VIDEO GAMES

PokéPark 2: Wonders Beyond – A sequel to the original Poképark Wii title. An adorable game directed at kids.

Pokémon Conquest (DS) – Pokémon Conquest is a tactical, turn–based, strategy game that is very similar to the Fire Emblem games. If you haven't tried a tactical game, this is a great game to start with.

Pokémon Black 2 and Pokémon White 2 (DS) – These two RPG games are actually sequels rather than remakes. The story here takes place 2 years after Black and White.

ANIME

Season 15 – Black & White: Rival Destinies, 49 episodes – Ash, Iris and Cilan continue exploring in the Unova region. The gang decides to compete in the Pokémon World Tournament Junior Cup. Team Rocket is still causing trouble.

Kyurem vs. The Sword of Justice – This is the 15th Pokémon movie. Ash, Iris and Cilan are on a train when Ash spots an injured Keldeo. Ash has to help solve another mystery.

2013

TRADING CARD GAME

B&W Plasma Storm – This set marks the debut of Team Plasma. Plasma cards featured a blue border instead of the typical yellow border.

B&W Plasma Freeze – Continues the Plasma trend with strong cards like Team Plasma Ball.

B&W Plasma Blast – The last Plasma set. This set brought in cards to counteract some of the strong Plasma cards that were introduced in earlier sets.

B&W Legendary Treasures – Legendary Treasures was mostly a reprint set, featuring many of the biggest cards in the Black & White era.

VIDEO GAMES

Pokémon Mystery Dungeon: Gates to Infinity (3DS) – Another installment of Nintendo's Pokémon Dungeon Crawler series.

Pokémon Rumble U (Wii U) – This was the first Pokémon game for the Wii U. This is a sequel to the Pokémon Rumble Blast game.

Pokémon X and Pokémon Y (3DS) – X and Y introduced 72 new Pokemon (Generation VI). Pokémon X and Y lead players into the Kalos region for the first time.

ANIME

Season 16 – Black & White Adventures in Unova and Beyond, 45 episodes. – Ash competes in the Unova League Championship. Ash meets a boy named N, who joins Ash's party along with Iris and Cilan.

Pokémon the Movie: Genesect and the Legend Awakened – This is the 16th Pokémon movie. This movie takes place in New York City. Mewtwo is back and comes to the aid of Ash, Iris and Cilan.

2014

TRADING CARD GAME

XY – This is the first expansion to feature Fairy–type Pokémon and Mega Evolution Pokémon.

XY Flashfire – Brought in many cards that made Evolution Decks more powerful.

XY Furious Fists – Gave Fighting decks a ton of support with cards like Fighting Stadium and Strong Energy.

Phantom Forces – This set featured Team Flare and Pokémon Spirit Link cards.

VIDEO GAMES

Pokémon Omega Ruby and Alpha Sapphire (3DS) – Remakes of the original Ruby and Sapphire games. Some of the small towns from the original games have grown into big cities. There are also some Mega Evolutions that were not in the original games.

Pokémon Art Academy (3DS) – An educational art game for the 3DS. The game teaches you how to draw a variety of Pokémon characters on your 3DS.

ANIME

Season 17 – Pokémon the Series: XY, 48 episodes. Ash and Pikachu begin their travels in the Kalos region. Ash makes new friends in Clemont, an inventor, and his little sister Bonnie. They are soon joined by Serena, a Pokémon Performer in training.

Diancie and the Cocoon of Destruction – The 17th Pokémon movie. The Pokémon Diancie enlists the help of Ash, Serena, Clemont and Bonnie to protect and restore the Heart Diamond.

2015

TRADING CARD GAME

XY Primal Clash – Introduced the new Ancient Traits mechanic.

XY Roaring Skies – This set had a big focus on Colorless Pokémon with strong cards.

Ancient Origins – Features the first appearance of the Mythical Pokémon Hoopa.

BREAKthrough – This set introduced Pokémon BREAK and Stadium cards with two different effects.

VIDEO GAMES

Pokémon Super Mystery Dungeon (3DS) – Another installment of Nintendo's Pokémon Dungeon Crawler series.

ANIME

Season 18 – Pokémon the Series: XY Kalos Quest, 45 episodes – Ash and his friends continue their journey through the Kalos region.

Pokémon the Movie: Hoopa and the Clash of Ages – The 18th Pokémon movie. Ash and his friends Serena, Clement and Bonnie travel to the desert and encounter a legendary Pokémon named Hoopa.

2016

TRADING CARD GAME

XY BREAKPoint – Brought us more powerful Pokémon BREAK and Pokémon–EX.

Generations – Another reprint set that appears exclusively in bundles.

XY Fates Collide – This set brought Zygarde and BREAK Evolutions of Basic Pokémon to the TCG.

XY Steam Siege – This set included Pokémon–EX, Pokémon BREAK, as well as some dual type Pokémon.

XY Evolutions – This set ended the XY era. Many cards are reprints, but there are some new cards.

VIDEO GAMES

Pokémon Red / Blue / Yellow for (3DS) – Released as part of the Pokémon 20th–anniversary event. These games are basically re–releases of the original games, not remakes.

Pokémon Pokken Tournament (Wii U) – An Arcade Style Fighting game for the Wii U.

Pokémon Go – A fantastic free app for Smart Phone users. This is an augmented reality mobile game that allows players with GPS to locate, capture, train and battle Pokémon which appear as if they are in the player's real–world location.

Pokémon Sun & Pokémon Moon (3DS) – These games introduced Pokémon from the Alola region (Generation VII). These games had Battle Royale, which allowed four players to battle one another at the same time.

ANIME

Season 19 – XYZ, 48 Episodes – The gang begin their journey to Snowbelle City for Ash's final gym match before qualifying for the Kalos league.

Volcanion and the Exquisite Magearna – The 19th Pokémon movie. Ash and Volcanion somehow get invisibly linked together through the powers of a mysterious belt. Serena, Clement, Bonnie and Team Rocket appear.

2017

TRADING CARD GAME

Sun & Moon (S&M) – This set introduces GX cards, and Pokémon from Alola region.

S&M Guardians Rising – This set brings us more Alolan Pokémon and more GX cards.

S&M Burning Shadows – More Alolan Pokémon, GX cards and some Team Skull trainers.

S&M Crimson Invasion – Ultra Beasts from the video games debut with this set.

VIDEO GAMES

Pokkén Tournament DX (Switch) – The arcade style fighting game becomes available on the Nintendo Switch.

Pokémon Ultra Sun and Ultra Moon (3DS) – These are enhanced versions of the original Sun & Moon video games.

ANIME

Season 20 – Sun & Moon, 43 Episodes – Ash and Pikachu travel to the Alola region. They meet Professor Kukui, Samson Oak, Kiawe, Lana, Mallow, Sophocles and Lillie. Team Rocket and Team Skull are around to cause trouble.

Pokémon the Movie: I Choose You! – The 20th Pokémon Movie – This movie is a reimaging of the first Pokémon Anime episode. It's like an alternate universe of Pokémon.

2018

TRADING CARD GAME

S&M Ultra–Prism – The first set to feature Prism Star cards. Prism star cards go to the Lost Zone when discarded. Cynthia is amazing card from this set.

S&M Forbidden Light – This set has more Pokémon–GX cards, Prism Star cards, and more Pokémon cards from the Alola and Kalos regions.

S&M – Celestial Storm – This set feature more Prism Star cards, GX cards, and Ultra Beasts cards.

S&M Lost Thunder – The chase card here is the Rainbow Rare Lugia GX card.

VIDEO GAMES

Detective Pikachu (3DS) – This game is almost like an animated storybook. An easy game with a fun storyline. This game was the basis of the Detective Pikachu movie.

Let's Go, Pikachu! and Let's Go, Eevee! (Switch) – These games are a new take on the standard RPG Pokémon games. The games are a little easier, and feature a new Pokémon Go style catch mechanism.

Super Smash Bros. Ultimate (Switch) – Another fantastic Smash Bros. game. Greninja, Jigglypuff, Lucario, Mewtwo, Pichu, Plkachu and Pokémon Trainer are all playable characters in this version.

ANIME

Season 21 – Sun & Moon: Ultra Adventures, 49 episodes – Ash and his classmates (Lillie, Lana, Mallow, Kiawe, and Sophocles) continue their adventures at the Pokémon school in the Alola region.

The Power of Us – The 21st Pokémon Movie. Ash and the gang attend the annual Wind Festival in Fula City. The festival celebrates the Legendary Pokémon Lugia. Threats occur, and someone has to save the day.

2019

TRADING CARD GAME

S&M Team Up – This set introduced the Tag Team Pokémon–GX mechanic, with two Pokémon on one powerful card.

S&M Unbroken Bonds – A huge expansion with over 200 cards. This expansion focuses heavily on Generation 1 Pokémon.

S&M Unified Minds – Another huge expansion with over 230 cards! Reset Stamp was a powerful card here.

S&M Cosmic Eclipse – The final set from the Sun & Moon series. This set had the first appearance of Tag Team Supporters. At 271 cards, this is currently the largest Pokémon TCG set ever released.

VIDEO GAMES

Pokémon Sword and Shield (Switch) – Sword and Shield introduced Generation VIII Pokémon from the Galar region. These games blend ideas from Let's Go Pikachu and the older RPGs. These are the first mainline Pokémon RPG games released on the Switch.

ANIME

Season 22 – Sun & Moon: Ultra Legends, 54 episodes – Ash and his classmates finish their adventures in the Alola region. Ash meets a new rival named Hau.

Mewtwo Strikes Back–Evolution – This is the 22nd Pokémon movie. It is a CGI remake of the first Pokémon movie.

2020

TRADING CARD GAME

Sword & Shield (SnS) – The first set featuring cards from the Galar region. SnS introduced Pokémon–V and Pokémon–VMAX. Sword and Shield also introduced the "Regulation Mark" to determine card legality in Pokémon Tournaments.

SnS Rebel Clash – The second set from Sword and Shield.

SnS Darkness Ablaze – The third set from Sword & Shield has the highly coveted Charizard VMAX card.

KEY SnS Vivid Voltage – This set introduced "Amazing Pokémon" cards to the TCG. These cards have watercolor rainbow art symbols on them. There are six Amazing Pokémon cards this set.

VIDEO GAMES

Pokémon Mystery Dungeon: Rescue Team DX (Switch) – This is a remake of the Red and Blue Mystery Dungeon games. This version adds Mega Evolved Pokémon, improved graphics and improved gameplay.

ANIME

Season 23 – Journeys, 48 Episodes – Ash visits the new Galar region for the first time, but also visits all regions from previous seasons. Ash travels with Goh. Goh dreams of catching Mew. Several characters from previous seasons return during this season.

Secrets of the Jungle – This is the 23rd Pokémon movie. This is like a Tarzan–Pokémon mashup. Ash actually mentions his father in this movie. As of this writing, this is the last Pokémon movie.

2021

TRADING CARD GAME

SnS Battle Styles – This set introduced the "Battle Styles" mechanic. Pokémon cards can carry either Single Strike Style or Rapid Strike Style.

SnS Chilling Reign – There are some nice cards for collectors in this set, including Galarian Moltres and Blaziken VMAX.

SnS Evolving Skies – This set reintroduced Dragon type Pokémon after a bit of a hiatus. Keep an eye out for Umbreon VMAX.

SnS Fusion Strike – A huge set with 264 cards. This set introduces the Fusion Strike Battle Style.

VIDEO GAMES

New Pokémon Snap (Switch) – This is a new adventure based on the original Pokémon Snap from the Nintendo 64. There is some good storytelling here. It is a great reinvention of the original game.

Pokémon Brilliant Diamond and Shining Pearl (Switch) – These are enhanced remakes of Diamond and Pearl. There are 493 Pokémon from the first 4 generations to catch. A good piece of nostalgia for the Switch.

ANIME

Season 24: Master Journeys, 42 episodes – Ash, Goh, and Chloe travel across all eight regions, from Kanto to Galar. Again, several characters from previous seasons return during this season.

2022

TRADING CARD GAME

SnS Astral Radiance – This set introduced Radiant cards. These are usually Basic Pokémon with powerful attacks.

SnS Lost Origin – This set featured the return of the Lost Zone mechanic.

SnS Silver Tempest – This is the final expansion of the Sword & Shield Series.

VIDEO GAMES

Pokémon Legends: Arceus (Switch) – This is an Action RPG rethinking of traditional Pokémon RPG games. Catching Pokémon is not turn-based. You capture Pokémon in real time, and the game is more difficult than your usual Pokémon fare. Arceus has more of an open-world feel compared to older games as well.

Pokémon Scarlet and Violet (Switch) – Pokémon Scarlet and Pokémon Violet are the first true open-world RPGs in the Pokémon series. This game takes you to the Paldea region with Generation IX Pokémon. A total of 103 new creatures are added with these expansions.

ANIME

Season 25: Ultimate Journeys – This is the 25th season of the Pokémon anime. It was announced in December 2022, that this would be the final season for Ash and Pikachu as main characters. Brock and Misty return.

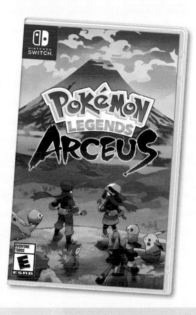

2023

TRADING CARD GAME

Scarlet and Violet – We are writing this book in early 2023. The Pokémon TCG: Scarlet & Violet expansion will launch worldwide in March 2023. Yellow borders on Pokémon TCG cards will become gray to match the cards released in Japan. Pokémon-EX make their return as well.

ANIME

It has been announced that a new anime series will premiere in 2023 and will take place in Paldea. The story will follow new heroes Liko and Roy. It will also feature the Paldea Pokémon Sprigatito, Fuecoco and Quaxly from the Pokémon Scarlet and Pokémon Violet video games, as well as the Legendary Pokémon Rayquaza in its Shiny form.

Pokémon Anime

Ash's Story Arcs

By Angel Pelaez

We have a look back at 25 years of Pokemon anime. Which seasons were our favorites? Which seasons were your favorites? Let's take a stroll down memory lane.

If you have not heard already, Ash is leaving the Pokémon anime, and he is taking Pikachu, Team Rocket and the rest of the timeless cast with him. At this point, we still do not know much about the future of the series besides the appearance of a couple new protagonists. But it is worth looking back and remembering a bit about all these years of Pokémon history.

I remember being 12 years old when the anime premiered. I was ready and so excited about finally being able to watch the adventures of Ash and Pikachu. So, I prepared and even recorded around 300 episodes on VHS before giving it up (I'm grateful for the internet and streaming platforms). But I stuck with the anime all these years, and followed Ash along this very long journey. Right now, while I'm writing this, his very final story arc of 11 episodes is airing on Japanese television. So, you could say I am also writing this with a pinch of nostalgia.

So let us look back and take a look at each one of the story arcs featuring Ash Ketchum from Pallet Town. Be warned as there will be some spoilers, but I will try to avoid them as much as possible. I'll be mentioning memorable characters, Pokémon and some of the main events on each arc, but there may be some details missed or skipped.

And with that, let us look back at this journey that has taken us all more than 25 years.

Indigo League
(82 episodes, 1997-1999)

This story arc introduced us to Ash Ketchum, a young boy from Pallet Town who is finally old enough to get his first Pokémon from Professor Oak and start his own journey to become a Pokémon master. Of course, things do not go as smoothly as planned and Ash oversleeps, arriving late to his appointment with destiny and receiving a troublesome Pokémon: Pikachu. They have a very rocky start to their adventure, and find their first companion in Misty after Ash borrowed and wrecked her bike escaping some pesky Spearow.

Misty sticks with Ash until he can replace her bike, and they encounter the villainous trio who would stick with them for over 25 years too: Jessie, James and Meowth, the least competent and most charismatic members of Team Rocket. Capturing that Pikachu would become their life mission and they would try it on every opportunity they would encounter after this.

Coming back to his primary objective, Ash decides to challenge the 8 gym leaders of the Kanto region in order to participate in the Pokémon League Tournament. Ash challenges the Pewter City gym leader Brock first, and Ash wins his first badge. Brock decides to join the adventure as well and the original trio of trainers travel across the Kanto region, challenging more gyms, encountering more Pokémon and forging a lifetime friendship.

After collecting all 8 badges, Ash enters the Indigo League, reaching a top 16 position after losing with his friend Richie. Gary Oak - Ash's original rival - also loses the championship.

This arc had a lot of memorable stories, such as the one behind Meowth's ability to speak. We also catch a glimpse of Giovanni using Mewtwo to defeat Gary. The Indigo League was the beginning of a painfully long trainer journey for Ash. This was a season for beginnings, and one that didn't disappoint at all.

Orange League
(36 episodes, 1999)

Ash and company return to Pallet Town and Oak asks for a favor: to meet Professor Ivy in the Orange Islands and retrieve the mysterious GS Ball, a unique kind of Pokéball that cannot be opened. Ash travels to these islands and he decides to join the local tournament while he's visiting.

Brock decides to stay with Professor Ivy, but his place in Ash's entourage is quickly filled with Tracey. Tracey is an artist whose dream is to meet Professor Oak, so he decides to tag along with Ash and Misty to make this happen upon their return to Pallet Town.

36 Episodes of Tropical Pokémon Adventures on 3 Discs!

This season is brief but full of great moments as Ash captures some memorable and powerful Pokémon, including a Lapras that also serves as means of transport across these islands and one of Ash's many Tauros.

The tournament holds special importance because it is also the first time we see Ash as a champion. Ash defeats Drake in a heated battle against a very powerful team with Pokémon such as Ditto and Dragonite.

After becoming the Orange Islands Champion, Ash & Company return to Pallet Town, where Tracey's dream comes true as he finally meets with Professor Oak. He is so passionate about Oak's work that he decides to stay working at the lab as an assistant. Shortly after, Brock rejoins Ash's team.

It's also worth noting that the Orange Islands do not exist in any of the Pokémon games so far. But they could be a reference to the Sevii Islands.

This arc also served as a very brief and subtle introduction to the Johto region as the mystery of the GS ball would extend well into the next story arc.

Pokémon: Johto League
(158 episodes, 1999-2002)

This arc includes the *Johto Journeys*, *Johto League Champions* and *Master Quest* seasons.

This arc shows the first time Ash travels to a whole new region as he meets with new and exciting Pokémon and characters. At this point, Ash's original Pokémon team was pretty much disbanded too. But he gets to meet and catch some great Pokémon, including the starter trio of this region, Heracross and an amazing shiny Noctowl.

The GS Ball argument keeps developing as Ash gets a new request to bring this very special ball to a Pokéball expert in Johto: Kurt, to discover once and for all if he could crack the mystery and finally open the GS Ball (spoilers: this did not happen). Another motivation for Ash to make this trip was to meet with Gary, who was again a step ahead of him exploring this new region.

Ash challenges and defeats some of the best-written and acted gym leaders. Everyone from Bugsy to Clair presents a worthy challenge and some amazing Pokémon battles. Ash gets to solve some mysteries involving the legendary Pokémon Lugia and gets all the gym badges, as expected. Then, he joins the Johto League Championship for another shot at glory.

He does great defeating Gary in an epic battle (even making Gary question his own motives). However, in his match against a skilled Pokémon trainer from the Hoenn region named Harrison, Ash loses against some Pokémon he has never seen before, namely Kecleon and Blaziken. Ash gets eliminated from the tournament, but finds a new motivation to travel to yet another region to catch and battle new and exciting Pokémon. This is how he decides to travel to the Hoenn region.

As soon as Ash returns to Pallet Town, Misty abandons the team to take care of the Cerulean City Gym. Brock also goes back to his family in Pewter City, and Ash leaves to a brand new region for a fresh start with Pikachu.

This was a season full of excitement. All of the new Pokémon this season had a great personality and we had some of the best battles occurring in this arc. When it ended, it truly felt like a fresh start for Ash: no comrades and no Pokémon by his side except for Pikachu.

As a final note about this arc, I still believe this had the best opening song of all the series. Do you remember it?

Hoenn League
(132 episodes, 2002-2005)

This arc includes the *Advanced*, *Advanced Challenge* and the first half of the *Advanced Battle* seasons.

To everyone's surprise, Brock rejoins Ash, and they also meet two new partners: May and her little brother Max. They tag along for the trip while going on parallel adventures, as May decides to become a Pokémon coordinator joining different Pokémon contests across the region. May gains experience and we learn about another side of Pokémon we have never seen before, one that does not involve battling. She needs 5 different ribbons in order to participate in the Hoenn Grand Festival.

Meanwhile Ash does his thing and challenges the 8 gym leaders of the region. We get to meet some great gym leaders such as Roxanne, Flannery and Normal (who actually defeated Ash before losing a rematch).

This arc also introduces some of the best Pokémon Ash has ever captured in terms of personality and development. I really think that Corphish and Torkoal did a lot for the show, and Treecko evolved into one of Ash's most powerful Pokémon. I also need to mention the great relationship between Phanpy and Pikachu.

This is the region when Ash gets to meet Team Aqua versus Team Magma, whose motives are a bit different from what we were used to. This is a pretty great story arc thanks to the strong writing. These teams unleash Kyogre and Groudon, and Ash gets caught in this legendary struggle. Ash has to help resolve this conflict to get back into his gym challenge.

May gets to participate in the Grand Festival, achieving a very respectable Top 8 standing, which is the same result Ash gets in the Hoenn League Championship. Ash is ultimately defeated by a very powerful trainer named Tyson, who ends up being the champion.

This was a memorable arc because it introduced new ideas. It showed that Pokémon training could take a very different route if you decide to become a coordinator. But it also introduced Max, a great support character that developed really well thanks to his devotion and love towards Pokémon. Max's young age prevented him from becoming a Pokémon trainer just yet. I think this worked nicely and set some hopes for the future (but we all know there is no such thing as aging in Ash Ketchum's world).

The introduction of a couple different villain teams also led to some fantastic development on the legendary mini-story arc for this season. When it ended, we did not really get a sense of closure because Ash's adventures with this team of companions and Pokémon were far from over, there was still a new frontier to conquer, and it was closer to home than expected.

Kanto Battle Frontier
(61 episodes, 2005-2006)

This arc includes the second half of the *Advanced Battle* season.

The gang goes back to Kanto, where Ash gets invited to take part in a new and exciting adventure: the Battle Frontier, a high-difficulty challenge (at least that is what it was in the games) where he needs to battle highly skilled trainers called Frontier Brains to get all the Frontier Symbols.

This is where Ash even gets to test his skills against legendary Pokémon. Articuno becomes one of the most memorable battles of this arc. Ash knows about its power, so he decides to call for Charizard, interrupting its training at Charicific Valley. And oh boy, was it worth it. It was a great battle, quite difficult for Charizard despite the type advantage, but Ash does get the victory and the chance to keep going in this new adventure.

The rest of Ash's battles go smoothly — that is, until he has to face Pyramid King Brandon. Ash gets defeated by a Registeel once, but gets another chance at a rematch and decides to bring Charizard, Bulbasaur and Squirtle to this new challenge. They join Pikachu for another shot against Brandon's

team of very powerful Pokémon, including Regice. Ash's team finally comes up on top of this quite difficult challenge.

After this victory, Ash gets offered a position as Frontier Brain, which he declines, opting instead to continue his journey to become a Pokémon master.

May also enters her own Kanto challenge to get 5 new ribbons, giving her a shot at the Kanto Grand Festival, achieving a very respectable Top 4 position.

There is also a very cool moment here as May and Ash battle for a ribbon before parting ways. It was a very close match, but ultimately Ash gets his Sceptile to split the ribbon in half, declaring a tie and saying goodbye to May as she continues walking her own path.

Ash then gets another chance to battle Gary and a new Pokémon of his: Electivire. Ash learns about the Sinnoh region and the exciting new Pokémon he can meet and capture there. Of course, our boy decides to go on another trip to a new region with some exciting new challenges.

This arc is short but very fulfilling. It's exciting in many ways as it references the Battle Frontier from the Pokémon games, which is one of the most difficult activities even to this day. The small number of episodes also means there is a lot of action and very little time wasted.

It was also a great arc for nostalgia as Charizard does make a big difference throughout this one. It made one thing clear: Ash would obliterate all of his challenges if he decided to stick with a team (or at least a few Pokémon) throughout seasons.

Saying goodbye to May also held quite the meaning. May became a beloved character and felt better suited for the show than Misty in many ways. Overall, it was a great way to focus on high action battles before slowing things down again as we transitioned to a new generation.

Diamond & Pearl
(191 episodes, 2006-2010)

This arc includes the seasons *Diamond & Pearl*, *Diamond & Pearl: Battle Dimension*, *Diamond & Pearl: Galactic Battles* and *Diamond & Pearl: Sinnoh League Victors*.

Ash decides to leave all of his Pokémon, except for Pikachu and a recently captured Aipom, before departing to the Hoenn Region. Upon arrival, he meets with Brock and a new partner: Dawn, an enthusiastic young girl who wishes to follow her mother's footsteps and become a great Pokémon coordinator.

The gang also meets with a new rival: Paul, whose methods and ideologies regarding Pokémon training are far colder and more cruel than Ash's. Paul even goes as far as to abandon his Chimchar for being too weak, but Ash touches the little Pokémon's heart and gets him to join the team alongside other great Pokémon such as Turtwig and Starly.

Ash's gym challenge goes well up until his 5th badge, where he pauses due to a reunion with May and a new invite to participate as a Pokémon coordinator by Pokémon League Champion Wallace.

When Ash resumes his gym challenge, it all goes smoothly. Then he meets a new rival: Barry. As his Pokémon Gym Challenge progresses, he trades his Aipom for Dawn's Buizel and catches a Gligar that evolves into Gliscor later on. Both are great additions for his team.

Ash has a great level of determination in his remaining gym battles, showing some maturity that we didn't get to see before. There is also a mini arc including the beloved character Looker and the legendary Pokémon of this generation. Team Galactic was never a particularly interesting organization, but it was a nice mini story arc.

Ash enters the Sinnoh Pokémon League and decides to call some of his old Pokémon to aid him (so you could say things were getting serious). He doesn't get to battle Barry, but finally beats Paul with the help of a now fully evolved Infernape. However, he couldn't foresee the participation of Tobias, a very strong Pokémon trainer who even used a couple Legendaries: Darkrai and Latios. Ash does his best in this battle against this great challenge but ultimately loses, reaching a Top 4 position.

The end of this season also marks the end of an era since Ash says goodbye to Dawn, who achieves a very impressive second place at the Sinnoh Grand Festival and wishes to continue with her own path. Ash also parts ways with his oldest friend Brock for the very last time, as Brock now seeks to become a Pokémon doctor.

This was a great arc for those looking for great Pokémon battles. The team that Ash assembled really looked like one you could use for the games, and his strategies and techniques were a lot more polished this time around.

Best Wishes
(88 Episodes, 2010-2011)

This arc is also known as *Black & White*.

Ash gets an invitation from Professor Oak to visit the Unova Region, and you know our boy would never refuse such an offer. Upon arrival, an incident with Team Rocket and Zekrom prevents Pikachu from using electric attacks for a while, which is an interesting moment in the anime. This incident also leads to Ash losing his first battle against a new rival named Trip.

As expected, Ash decides to join the Unova Pokémon League and meets a couple of new companions for this adventure: Iris, a very talented dragon Pokémon trainer, and Cilan, one of the 3 Striaton City Gym leaders and Pokémon Connoisseur. Both of them fit in very well, as they feel similar to Brock and Misty, but they also develop unique personalities throughout the next few arcs.

Ash captures the trio of starter Pokémon from this region, something that had not happened since the Johto region. He also gets a few more interesting Pokémon and hatches a Scraggy from an egg, which was a very nice addition to his team for the season. This was also a season that really focused on Ash's Pokémon as individuals, their strengths and the value they offered to the team. Ash kept on challenging and defeating gym leaders, often having better development than other characters. They meet a lot of trainers and battle a lot throughout this arc.

Ash starts his gym challenge in this new region and faces some great gym leaders, such as Elesa, who has always been a fan favorite and didn't disappoint in her anime adaptation. This was also the arc where the Battle Subway is introduced, a familiar location for all videogame fans.

A very cool fact about this arc is that it served as base for other stories mostly within the same region, so we got a bit more time to get hooked by the story that was slowly developing for Ash, his Pokémon and his new companions who grew to be fan-favorites.

Best Wishes 2
(24 Episodes, 2011-2012)

This arc is also known as *Black & White: Rival Destinies.*

As Ash continues his journey to get the remaining 5 gym leader badges from this region, he is forced to take a break to help with a crisis that could destroy the entire Unova region: Giovanni, the powerful and evil Team Rocket leader, unleashes two very powerful legendary Pokémon: Tornadus and Thundurus, and Ash and company are in charge of finding and summoning Landorus to keep the balance and prevent total annihilation from happening.

Things go well, as expected, and Ash finally gets to resume his adventure. These prove to be difficult battles that help Ash's Pokémon get stronger and evolve, namely Boldore, Unfeazant and Pignite.

Ash makes time to participate in a couple more events to keep things interesting: He participates in a race to the top of Celestial Tower, where he gets second place, and the Donamite Tournament, where he gets to the semi-finals.

This is also the arc where Ash gets to face Tepig's original trainer and the remainder of Unova's gym leaders. It is a short arc, so there is a lot of action and a special focus on Pokémon battling, which is great. There is also one mini arc happening involving the legendary trio, again, and Meloetta.

Overall, this arc was short but sweet, building on what was set up in the last season and developing expectations for the next one.

Best Wishes 2: Episode N
(14 Episodes, 2012-2013)

This arc is also known as *Black & White: Adventures in Unova.*

After a couple story arcs, Ash finally joins the Unova Pokémon League. Unfortunately, this is a very short arc, so while there is a lot of action, it all feels rushed and there are not many memorable battles or rivals that could really develop properly. Ash places in the Top 8, so this is definitely one of the most difficult championships he has participated in.

There was a lot of discussion around why he has a relatively bad performance despite having a great gym challenge, such as the decision not to recall more Pokemon to the team. But these are topics for another day.

Ash meets a very interesting guy named N and Ash learns about Team Plasma and their evil plans involving the other legendary of the region: Reshiram. Despite N having different ideas about the concept of Pokémon and humans being able to coexist as equals, N and Ash form a great team that manages to overcome the crisis and defeat Team Plasma together.

It certainly feels like there was a lot happening in this very short arc. I would have liked more time and better development. These episodes are great if you are familiar with the Black & White Pokémon games and the mythology contained in these, but for younger or less knowledgeable audiences, it certainly felt like they were missing something here. N is of course a very interesting character with a deep story and interesting ideas, but it didn't quite connect deeply with Ash's journey.

Best Wishes: Decolora Adventure
(23 Episodes, 2013)

This arc is also known as *Black & White: Adventures in Unova and Beyond*.

When it is time for Ash to go back home from Unova, he gets some tickets to the Queen Decolore cruise, with a planned route that passes through the Decolore Islands before a final destination in Viridian City, back in Kanto.

This is another short arc that introduced Alexa, a reporter from the Kanto region. It also has a nice comeback from Claire, the Blackthorn City Gym leader all the way back in Johto, who is on a mission to capture a shiny Druddigon.

This is the second archipelago region that Ash explores, but it is far from what the Orange Islands adventure was. This region is home to Pokémon originally found in Kanto, Johto, Hoenn, Sinnoh and Unova, and I think it represented a great opportunity to catch and train a wide variety of Pokémon, but unfortunately no main character in this arc catches a single Pokémon, which felt like a missed opportunity.

The Complete Season

At the end of this cruise and upon their arrival in Kanto, Ash says goodbye to Cilan and Iris as they both decide to continue their journey to the Johto region. Ash heads to Pallet Town accompanied by Alexa, leaving for the Kalos region the next day.

Despite the missed opportunities in this arc, this served as a moment to slow the storylines down after 3 arcs and several seasons of mostly non-stop action. This arc offered a sense of closure for Ash's companions and this adventure in Unova while offering a glimpse of what was next in the future of the Pokémon series.

XY
(98 Episodes, 2013-2015)

This arc includes the *XY* and *XY Kalos Quest* seasons.

Ash travels to the Kalos region to compete in the Pokémon League and continues pursuing his dream of becoming a Pokémon Master. He meets and befriends some new companions too: siblings Bonnie and Clemont, as well as his childhood friend Serena, who has always had a crush on him (this is important later on, I promise).

Ash starts his adventures with these new teammates and captures Froakie and Fletchling. Both of these Pokemon would grow and evolve to become the core of Ash's team in this region. He also has some great gym battles that earn him his first few medals.

Then the gang gets to take a break to assist the Pokémon Summer Camp organized by Professor Sycamore where he meets Shauna, Trevor and Tierno.

As Ash resumes his gym challenge, he meets and battles with Korrina, who is not only a great gym leader, but also has a fantastic personality and teaches Ash about Mega Evolution. This knowledge would accompany him for the rest of his journey and way beyond this arc.

Froakie evolves into Frogadier and Ash also gets to face and learn from Ramos. Then Ash adopts a Goomy and

forms a very strong bond with it that causes it to evolve rather quickly into Sliggoo and Goodra shortly after.

Clemont is actually Lumiose City's gym leader, so when he sees the progress Ash is making in the region, he decides to split from the team temporarily to train and be the best version of himself for his battle with Ash. When this clash finally happens, they have a heated but honorable battle and Ash emerges victorious, earning his 5th gym badge.

Shortly after this, Ash resolves a conflict at Goodra's home and decides to leave this Pokémon behind so it can protect it. Hawlucha finds an egg and a Noibat hatches from it, joining Ash and his team in order to properly learn to fly.

There's also a mini arc that involves Moltres in which Ash's Fletchinder evolved into Talonflame in a heated battle against this powerful legendary Pokémon.

A lot happened in this arc, including the presence of legendary Pokémon from other regions, which was a very nice touch. It certainly felt like there was growth and development for Ash, his teammates and his Pokémon. Goodra´s story is a fantastic one, and it truly felt like each gym battle was tougher and more exciting than the previous one.

Ultimately, this arc was setting up something bigger, and it felt like a well-paced one after some rushed events during the last few arcs.

XYZ
(49 Episodes, 2015-2016)

The group finds a rather unique Pokémon and Bonnie names it Squishy. They learn that Squishy was being hunted by Team Flare, so they decide to stick with it as they travel so it can stay away from trouble.

This is where things get interesting as Frogadier evolves into Greninja and we discover that this Pokémon has a bond with Ash that is so powerful that it even gives it a special power that rivals Mega-Evolution (it would later be known as Ash-Greninja). They meet a new rival, Alain, and battle against his Charizard, putting up a good fight, but Alain ultimately claims the victory, forming a new friendly rivalry relationship between these two trainers.

The rest of Ash's Pokémon are also doing their best, and Noibat evolves into Noivern after yet another crisis involving Zapdos.

Ash learns that the power of Ash-Greninja comes with consequences as Ash faints while battling Alain again and has a vision about Greninja leaving him. Ash decides to be more careful when using this power.

This happens once more while facing the region's champion Diantha, and Ash starts to fear the power of the Ash-Greninja form. This fear, of course, becomes a burden for him and Greninja.

This fear costs Ash dearly as he loses his battle against Gym leader Wulfric. This fills Ash's mind with doubts, considering the Ash-Greninja form as a possible mistake. But Wulfric explains that the problem is a lack of faith and trust in this bond and form.

Ash splits from the team to spend some time alone in the Winding Woods and meditate about his future in Kalos. Serena finds him and gets into an argument with him that ultimately opens his eyes about his doubts. Greninja also looks for him and saves him from danger as they perfect the Ash-Greninja bond.

They return to their friends; Ash apologizes and thanks Serena for helping him out. The rematch against Wulfric finally happens and Ash gets his final gym badge just in time for the Kalos Pokémon League.

Ash enters the championship and gets to the semi-finals, when he recalls Goodra to lend a hand. Ash emerges victorious from his semi-final match and faces Alain in the final match of the tournament, and Alain becomes champion.

Team Flare attacks with another Pokémon similar to Squishy called Z-2 shortly after, and chaos ensues as everyone tries to find Squishy. Ash, Greninja and the rest of his Pokémon become hostages of Lysandre, Team Flare's boss, as he aims to use the power of the Ash-Greninja bond for his own purposes. It turns out Alain was also working for Lysandre, but without fully knowing the true intentions.

We then learn that Squishy is actually the legendary Pokémon Zygarde. Alain has a change of heart and helps Ash solve the situation. These heroic actions earn Ash and his Pokémon some Honor of Kalos medals.

Ash leaves Goodra again and faces yet another crisis with a Team Flare scientist that pretends to form a new Team Flare. This situation is quickly solved, but some negative energy remains as a consequence of Team Flare's efforts, so Squishy and Z-2 ask for Greninja's help to keep the situation under control. Greninja accepts and says goodbye to Ash.

As his Kalos adventure comes to an end, Ash also bids farewell to his friends (teasing a goodbye kiss with Serena) and goes back to Pallet Town.

This is an action-filled arc with lots of development for Ash as he faces his own fears. It feels like a very mature arc too if we compare it with all the previous ones. Another thing worthy of mentioning is the great results Ash gets from this region's tournament. You could certainly see that he has grown into a fine trainer now.

Sun & Moon
(146 Episodes, 2016-2019)

This arc includes the *Sun & Moon*, *Ultra Adventures* and *Ultra Legends* seasons.

This is one of the longest arcs and a lot of stuff happens. Ash goes on vacation to Alola with his mom, but quickly gets convinced to enroll in the local Pokémon School, where he meets Lillie, Mallow, Sophocles and Kiawe. He also meets Professor Kukui and stays at Kukui's place during his school days.

Ash learns about the legendary Pokémon of this region and encounters Tapu Koko, which shows Pikachu how to use the Z-Move Gigavolt Havoc with the help of a Z-Crystal. The crystal shatters because Ash has not passed an island trial, so he starts the Island Trial to earn another crystal.

Ash catches Rowlet and starts meeting Island Kahunas, solving different tasks and facing Totem Pokémon. He catches the Rockruff under Professor Kukui's care and battles Tapu Koko a few times to test his skills and progress.

Ash keeps traveling through the islands of the region and finds and catches Litten, who has a really touching backstory. Then Ash meets Gladion, Lillie's sister, and they quickly become friends and rivals. Rockruff evolves into Dusk Lycanroc, who is now also able to use Z-Moves. He then goes on a field trip to Kanto with his classmates, where he meets up with Brock and Misty, even battling with them.

Ash comes back to Alola and finds a strange Pokémon who stays under Lillie's care and gets nicknamed as Nebby. Lusamine, Lillie's mother, shows up and explains that Nebby is an Ultra Beast. We learn about these mysterious creatures and we also learn that they are the reason Lillie cannot touch a Pokémon due to a past trauma.

We are then introduced to Ultra Wormholes, passages to the dimension where Ultra Beasts live, and a big adventure around this concept involving Ash and his classmates takes place. Nebby evolves into Solgaleo during this time. The Ultra Guardian Corp. forms and Ash and company start a series of missions to capture Ultra Beasts in order to take them back home.

We learn about Professor Kukui's secret identity as the Masked Royal, a very skilled Pokemon Trainer/Wrestler with an Incineroar. We also learn about his intentions to establish a Pokémon League in Alola.

Ash captures an Ultra Beast of his own, Poipole, and learns about Necrozma. Lunala joins for an Ultra Guardians mission to free Solgaleo from Necrozma's possession and Poipole says goodbye to stay behind in its home dimension. Litten evolves into Torracat and starts becoming a very important part of Ash's team.

We have another mini-arc featuring Misty and Brock as they visit Alola as promised during their last encounter with the class. Ash captures the mysterious Pokémon Meltan. There's also another peculiar mini-arc that involves Celebi sending Ash and Torracat to the past to meet Kukui when he was a kid. It turns out Kukui's motivation to have a Pokémon League in Alola comes from Ash telling him all about his adventures in other regions during this period.

After a while, the Alola Pokémon League is ready and Ash and his friends enter it. The preliminary round is a battle royale match with 16 winners. Ash passes this test and defeats some great rivals such as Hau, Guzma and Gladion to become champion. Meltan evolves into Melmetal, providing even more power to Ash's Team.

A new Ultra Beast emerges unexpectedly — Naganadel, which is the evolved form of Ash's old Poipole — joins the team for the last exhibition match against The Masked Royal, whose secret identity is finally discovered.

Ash and Kukui's battle is epic. The battle is filled with Z-Moves, Ultra Beasts and even the surprising participation of Tapu Koko lending Kukui a hand. Ash emerges victorious from this battle as the first Alola Champion, proving himself against the strongest trainer this region has to offer. After this, Ash says goodbye to his Pokémon, leaving them under Kukui's care, and he goes back home to Pallet Town once more.

A lot happened during this arc, and the change of art style also gave new life to the Pokémon series. Ash winning his first Pokémon League was an amazing recognition after many years of trying, but his captures and the skills and knowledge he acquired in Alola really provided him the mindset and Pokémon to make this happen in a believable way.

Pocket Monsters
(72 Episodes, 2019-2023)

This arc includes the *Pokémon Journeys*, *Pokémon Master Journeys* and *Pokémon Ultimate Journeys* seasons.

This is the arc currently airing in the U.S., so I'll try to avoid details as much as I can, but be mindful of spoilers as I'll describe the end of this arc as it already aired in Japan.

This season starts off in a weird way as Ash gets to go to a new Pokémon Laboratory, but leaves to investigate a Lugia sighting in Vermilion City. He gets to know Goh, his companion for this arc, who is on a quest to catch all the Pokémon.

Together, they become assistants of Professor Cerise and go on some assessments for him. This new adventure takes them to Galar, where they start meeting and catching new Pokémon.

They come back and forth exploring all previous areas and meeting with old friends. Along this trip, Ash also gets to catch some impressive Pokémon such as Dragonite.

Shortly after, Ash learns about the World Coronation Series, a tournament for the very best Pokémon trainers in the world. Ash gets to watch a match between Lance (from the Kanto Elite Four) versus Leon (Pokémon Champion of Galar).

Ash learns about the Dynamax and Gigantamax phenomenon and helps out with some missions regarding this Galar-exclusive deal. Ash decides to join the World Coronation Series and has to battle some formidable rivals in order to climb up the rankings and secure a spot for the next one.

Ash catches Gengar and hatches a Riolu from an egg.

This happens while Ash starts winning his ranking matches against some impressive and tough Pokémon trainers from the past, such as Korrina and some new ones, such as Bea. He also keeps assembling an impressive team with the addition of a Galarian Farfetch'd.

Ash and Goh have some adventures that involve more legendary Pokémon, as well as some weird stuff happening with the Dynamax phenomenon. They face Chairman Rose because of his evil intentions involving Eternatus and save the Galar region along the way.

Ash enters the World coronation series with an impressive team (Pikachu, Dragonite, Gengar, Lucario, Sirfetch'd and Dracovish), and it's clear that the level of this competition is way higher than anything else he's ever participated in as his rivals are world renowned trainers and champions: Leon, Cynthia, Diantha, Steven, Lance, Alain and Iris.

The battles are fierce and Ash manages to reach the final match against Leon. This is most definitely the fiercest and best-animated battle Ash has ever had. There is Gigantamaxing, Z-Moves and Mega Evolution. And when the dust settled, Pikachu is the last Pokémon standing, earning Ash the title of World Champion.

Finally!

Pokémon: Aim to be a Pokémon Master!
(11 Episodes, 2023)

This is the last Hurrah for Ash and Pikachu, a miniseries that asks a simple question: what does it mean to be a Pokémon Master? Ash is already a world champion, the very best that no one ever was… so what's next? This mini-series aims to answer that question while meeting with old friends and Pokémon. The series is currently airing in Japan and I won't be telling you anything about it. It's very special, so I hope you watch it when you have the chance.

The Top 10 Cards
OF EVERY ERA

By Jason Klaczynski and Tord Reklev

In this segment, two Pokémon Trading Card Game champions break down the Top 10 cards of every era. We are not looking at the fanciest or the most expensive cards, but rather the cards players used to take down tournaments and win championships. Extra credit is given to cards that remained strong across multiple years and formats.

The first eight Top 10 lists, beginning with the iconic first generation of cards and ending at XY, are written by Jason Klaczynski. The final two lists, covering the top cards from the Sun & Moon and Sword & Shield eras, are written by Tord Reklev.

Jason is a 3-time World Champion and the 2015 US National Champion. He played competitively from 1999 through 2016, and now plays retro formats exclusively, which he writes about on his Retro Pokémon TCG blog: jklaczpokémon.com.

JASON KLACZYNSKI

Tord is a 4-time International Champion whose breakout season was in 2017, when he won the North American International Championship. Since then, Tord has dominated tournaments. You can follow him on Twitter at @TordReklev.

TORD REKLEV

READ ON!

Gen. 1
(1999–2000)

It was the Pokémon boom. Pokémon had finally made its way overseas from Japan and parents were scrambling to find stores that sold booster packs. We remember the earliest days of Pokémon cards for producing the coveted trio of Blastoise, Venusaur and Charizard, but when it came time to battle, it was powerful Basic Pokémon like Hitmonchan and Electabuzz, alongside a heavy arsenal of Trainer cards that were taking down tournaments.

10. Energy Removal (Base Set)

Pick an Energy and discard it. It was so simple, yet so effective. Part of the reason for its strength was that Energy Removal could be used alongside Super Energy Removal, which discarded two of your opponent's Energy cards. With this endless barrage of Energy-stripping Trainers, you could make attacking difficult for your opponent.

8. Lickitung (Jungle)

It didn't get the attention it deserved back in 1999 when it debuted, but the reality is Lickitung is the most effective stalling Pokémon there is in the earliest formats. That's because its simple ability to keep pecking the opponent for 10 damage would apply just enough pressure on your opponent to force them to spend cards. With 90 HP, Lickitung felt like it took forever to KO, and by the time you finally knocked one out, half of your deck might already be in the discard pile.

9. Chansey (Base Set)

120 HP and 1 retreat on a Basic Pokémon? Chansey's stats were so overpowered that when it got its art reprinted years later in XY Evolutions, they had to nerf it with a three retreat cost. (In comparison, every other Base Set Pokémon got a noticeable boost!) Chansey was not just great for stalling, but its Double-edge attack could be used to take out big attackers, like an 80 HP Wigglytuff.

7. Lass (Base Set)

Lass was really powerful hand disruption, shuffling away all the Trainer cards from each player's hand. This limited what a player could do during the following turns. When the Neo sets debuted, Lass became even stronger, as it was paired with Cleffa's Eeeeeeek attack to refuel the user's hand, making the hand disruption one-sided.

6. Gust of Wind (Base Set)

Gust of Wind allowed you to either pick off a Pokémon on your opponent's Bench for an easy Prize card, or to strand a Pokémon with a high Retreat Cost in the Active spot. An eternal element of the game, this card has received several reprints under different names over the years, but has remained an effective (and fun) strategy.

3. Scyther (Jungle)

The most versatile Pokémon of the early days, Scyther's solid HP, free retreat, and ability to attack for Colorless Energy allowed it to splash into just about any deck. It launched at the Jungle expansion, just in time to curb the power of the dominant Hitmonchan. But it also continued to see play in the years that followed, since its 30-damage Slash was an effective way to one-hit KO 30 HP Baby Pokémon that debuted in the Neo sets of the early 2000s.

5. Item Finder (Base Set)

Considering how many powerful Trainers existed in Pokémon's earliest sets (almost all of them in Base Set), anything that allowed you to recover them was automatically good. The fact that Item Finder allowed you to reuse Super Energy Removal to continuously wipe out two Energy cards at a time from your opponent's board agonized many opponents.

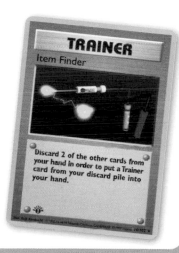

2. Super Energy Removal (Base Set)

No card has had such an impact on the game as Base Set's Super Energy Removal. If you ever attempted to build a deck around some powerful Evolved Pokémon with impressive attacks (like Charizard), Super Energy Removal would give you a quick reality check. This card single-handedly kept most cards in binders instead of decks. The unfortunate reality of Super Energy Removal is that if a Pokémon needed more than two Energy to attack, it probably wasn't going to make the cut. (And that was a lot of cards!)

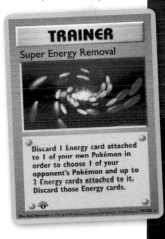

4. Double Colorless Energy (Base Set)

Considering you had to fight through a barrage of Energy Removals and Super Energy Removals to deliver any meaningful attacks, Double Colorless Energy was maxed out in many early Pokémon TCG decks, allowing players to deliver attacks like Scyther's Slash and Wigglytuff's Do the Wave for only two Energy cards.

1. Professor Oak (Base Set)

You could call Professor Oak the defining Trainer of the Pokémon TCG: it made the game what it was. The easy access to a new hand that Professor Oak provided enabled decks to do what they needed to, especially when it came to delivering aggression. It's why fast, aggressive decks dominated the earliest days of the TCG. But the fact that it came with a steep cost (discarding your entire hand), also made it fit perfectly into a game of strategy. It was up to the player to decide if pitching their hand was worth it.

Neo
(2000-2002)

It was the era of coin flips. Baby Pokémon quickly took the game over by storm (you'll see one in our #1 spot), slowing down what had become a crazy game of trying to beat your opponent as quickly as possible. With new tournament formats produced by Wizards of the Coast, we also finally saw some Stage 2 Pokémon being used in the top decks.

10. Dark Gengar (Neo Destiny)

Needing two coin flips to wake up meant your opponent's Pokémon was probably staying asleep. And that meant more uncontested attacks from Dark Gengar! Even 120 HP Pokémon could succumb to a series of Pull In attacks. But what made Dark Gengar even better was that it offered a way to pick off Baby Pokémon from your opponent's Bench without even needing a coin flip!

8. Feraligatr (Neo Genesis)

Feraligatr's massive Riptide attack was a force to be reckoned with in Pokémon's first Modified format, which rotated out the Energy Removal & Super Energy Removal Trainers that would have otherwise kept it in check. Using a variety of Trainers to replenish water in the discard pile, Feraligatr could deliver massive Riptide attacks that could one-hit KO any Pokémon you encountered.

9. Focus Band (Neo Genesis)

There was a time period where one-hit KOs dictated games. What better card, then, than Focus Band? Championships were won and lost on Focus Band coin flips. Focus Band was often attached to a player's most valuable Pokémon, but sometimes it was put on a Baby Pokémon to make the opponent need an additional coin flip to land a knockout.

7. Metal Energy (Neo Genesis)

The 10 damage Metal Energy reduced from attacks was a big deal, especially since it stacked in multiples. But what made Metal Energy even stronger is crafty tricks that allowed it to reduce self-damage by 20. This allowed Pokémon like Chansey to become monster attackers.

6. Gold Berry (Neo Genesis)

Before Gold Berry, players had to spend an Energy card with Super Potion to heal 40 damage. But Gold Berry had no such requirement; it was a free healing of 40 damage that triggered as soon as a Pokémon accumulated 40 damage. This was a big deal back in 2000–2002, when most attacks did less than 40 damage.

3. Murkrow (Neo Genesis)

The fact that Murkrow's Mean Look's effect lasted as long as Murkrow stayed active allowed Murkrow to permanently trap a variety of Pokémon. To make it even deadlier, it was combined with Pokémon like Slowking that prevented your opponent from escaping with Trainer cards. The icing on the cake, though? Murkrow's second attack could hit your opponent's bench. This meant you could strand a helpless Pokémon active, then deliver Feint Attacks until your opponent's Bench was completely wiped out.

5. Dark Crobat (Neo Destiny)

Since Dark Golbat's Pokémon Power dealt 10 damage, the sequence of evolving into Dark Golbat and then Dark Crobat meant you could bypass the pesky Baby rule and knock out one of your opponent's 30 HP Baby Pokémon without even needing to flip a coin. Considering how popular Baby Pokémon were in the Neo days, this was a big deal!

2. Slowking (Neo Genesis)

Under its original Japanese text, Slowking's Mind Games only worked when Slowking was active. However, due to a huge blunder by Wizards of the Coast, the Power was mistranslated to also work from the Bench, allowing players multiple Mind Games coin flips to stop their opponent's Trainers from being played. This inability to play Trainers resulted in a lot of quick and one-sided games. (It was eventually banned!)

4. Sneasel (Neo Genesis)

Sneasel had everything: solid HP, free retreat, no Weakness, a useful Resistance, and most importantly, a powerful 2-Energy attack. Factor in the extra 10 damage boost Darkness Energy gave Sneasel and Beat Up was usually landing a one-hit KO against the Pokémon on the receiving end of it.

1. Cleffa (Neo Genesis)

Quite possibly the best card of all time, Cleffa completely changed the way the Pokémon TCG was played. That's because in the year leading up to its release, the game was plagued with overpowered Trainers that could completely wipe away an opponent's hand as early as the first turn of the game. Cleffa was the cure to these short, disappointing games, offering players a way to recover a fresh hand of 7 cards for a single Energy. Even better, Cleffa made up for its low HP with the Baby Rule, which required your opponent to hit a coin flip to be able to attack it.

e-Card
(Expedition-Skyridge, 2002-2003)

e-Card is named after the e-Reader compatibility of cards. The e-Reader was an attachable device for GameBoy Advance that let you scan a barcode on your cards to activate mini games and Pokédex info. Totaling only three sets, and with no particularly impressive cards, it's no surprise that the e-Card era seems to be the most forgotten time period in the game.

10. Gengar (Expedition)

Gengar's Hide in Shadows allowed it to attack and then flee to safety on the Bench. This by itself was good, but its Chaos Move Poké-Power is what allowed you to wreak havoc on your opponent's board. You could heal damage from your side of the board while simultaneously bringing your opponent's Pokémon closer to knocked out.

8. Professor Elm's Training Method (Expedition)

The e-Card era placed a heavy emphasis on Evolved Pokémon, which is what made Professor Elm's Training Method so good. You couldn't do much in the format without evolving Pokémon, so this was a key card in many decks.

9. Metal Energy (Expedition, Aquapolis)

Metal Energy's −10 reduction was a big deal since attacks in the e-Card years still weren't dealing heavy amounts of damage. A Pokémon stacked with multiple Metal Energy was likely to survive several of your opponent's attacks.

7. Friend Ball (Skyridge)

There weren't a lot of ways to search out Pokémon that didn't require the use of your once-per-turn Supporter, but Friend Ball was one of them. It was particularly useful for finding Colorless Pokémon, since most decks you would encounter were themselves playing them.

6. Beedrill (Skyridge)

Paralysis and Poison just from evolving? Beedrill's Venom Spray was an incredibly strong Poké-Power, but what made Beedrill even better is the fact that you could use various Trainers and Energy cards to devolve Beedrill back to Kakuna, then re-evolve it later for a second use of Venom Spray. This was sure to drive your opponents mad!

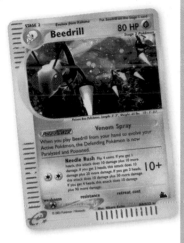

3. Oracle (Skyridge)

Setting yourself up for two good draws is definitely useful, but the true strength of Oracle came to the less patient players who found access to those cards right away. By combining Oracle with Poké-Powers like Porygon2's Backup or Delcatty's Energy Draw, players could locate two useful cards in their deck and immediately bring them into their hand.

5. Arcanine (Skyridge)

Arcanine's Energy Recharge could fuel up a White Flames attack out of nowhere. What made Arcanine even better was the fact that its Fire type allowed it to KO those otherwise difficult-to-KO Metal Pokémon like Scizor.

2. Scizor (Aquapolis)

Scizor was a deadly combination of both offense and defense. Each Metal Energy you attached to it not only reduced damage it took by 10, but also gave you an extra coin flip to add 20 damage to its Heavy Metal attack. By the time Scizor was tanked with multiple Metal Energies, there was little your opponent could do besides watch it mow down their Pokémon.

4. Copycat (Expedition)

Professor Oak's Research gave players a fresh hand of 5 cards, but Copycat was usually a better bet, especially in the age of Cleffa's Eeeeeeek attack, when your opponent would often have seven cards in their hand.

1. Furret (Aquapolis)

Furret's Scavenger Hunt allowed you to search out the strongest Energy cards, like Metal & Darkness Energy, to stack on to your Pokémon. It could also find those situational cards, like Warp Energy to escape a predicament or Boost Energy to launch a 3-Energy attack out of nowhere.

EX
(Ruby & Sapphire-Power Keepers, 2003-2007)

A beloved era of the game that produced skill-based and fun formats, the EX era is named for its introduction of Pokémon-ex, which were more powerful Pokémon that surrendered two Prize cards when knocked out. The EX era also marked the time period of the game where Pokémon transitioned from being produced by Wizards of the Coast to what is now The Pokémon Company International.

10. Electrode ex (FireRed LeafGreen)

Extra Energy Bomb gave up two Prize cards, but you hardly minded this in the EX era, since there were so many rewards for being behind in Prizes. You could use these Energy cards to fuel massive attacks that would otherwise take multiple turns to power up.

8. Pidgeot (FireRed LeafGreen)

Perhaps the greatest Ability of all time, Pidgeot's Quick Search gave its owner an enormous advantage of any card from your deck on every turn. Shortly after its debut in EX FireRed LeafGreen, several cards were printed to disable its Quick Search Poké-Power. Nonetheless, Pidgeot continued to see play, countering these counters. If you saw a match where one player had access to Quick Search and the other didn't, you would almost always see the player with Quick Search would emerge victorious.

9. Stantler (Unseen Forces)

Like most eras in Pokémon, the EX era put a heavy emphasis on Trainer cards. That's why Stantler's Push Away was so deadly. It could strip away Supporters, Rare Candy, or ways for your opponent to escape a stranded Pokémon. And it's not like Screechy Voice wasn't useful either!

7. Scramble Energy (Deoxys, Dragon Frontiers)

Trying to run your opponent over quickly often backfired in the EX era since there were so many cards that rewarded the player behind in Prizes. And what was the worst punishment you could receive for going too aggressive early in the game? A Scramble Energy-fueled attack that delivered a swift one-hit KO in response to your knockout.

6. Jirachi (Deoxys)

Jirachi's Wishing Star was one of the most popular ways to set up during the EX era. Needing no Energy, you could simply retreat to Jirachi, then begin hunting for the cards you needed to set up. If Jirachi stayed Asleep, there were a variety of ways to wake it up so it could use Wishing Star again on the next turn.

3. Holon Transceiver (Delta Species)

There were so many good Holon Supporters. Among the best of them were Holon Mentor to search out Basic Pokémon, Holon Adventurer & Scientist to draw cards, and Holon Researcher to search out Pokémon. Holon Transceiver allowed you to find whichever one of these was appropriate for the moment, and it even allowed you to pull a Supporter out of the discard pile to reuse it! Many decks in the EX era maxed out on this card as a reliable way to set up.

5. Windstorm (Crystal Guardians)

Players often relied on their own Stadium cards as a way to counter their opponent's, but for decks that didn't need too many of their own Stadium cards, Windstorm was an even better bet. That's because it doubled as a way to strip away your opponent's Pokémon Tools, including the pesky Cessation Crystal that disabled all Poké-Powers and Poké-Bodies.

2. Pow! Hand Extension
(Team Rocket Returns)

Pow! Hand Extension was basically a combination of two of the strongest Trainers from the game's past: Gust of Wind and Energy Removal. While it technically didn't remove Energy, there were ways you could do this. Pow could be used to snipe the strongest Pokémon from your opponent's bench. Many times, though, it was used to strand a weak Pokémon in the Active spot while you attacked your opponent's bench. Several decks relied on this card as an integral part of their strategy.

4. Holon's Castform (Holon Phantoms)

Holon's Castform's unique ability to provide two of any Energy allowed seemingly impossible attacks, like Lugia ex's 200-damage Elemental Blast, to be pulled off with ease. Since Holon's Castform was a Pokémon, you could now search out Energy the same way you searched out a Pokémon. And even better? It actually had a useful attack for setting up as well!

1. Rocket's Admin. (Team Rocket Returns)

In the first few turns, it delivered a respectable 6 cards to your hand. Late in the game, it stripped away your opponent's options, allowing you to deny them the cards needed to secure victory. Rocket's Admin. was not only incredibly powerful, but one of the most exciting and fun cards in the game, producing dramatic finishes. When timed just right, it allowed players to mount incredible comebacks. During its lifespan in competitive play, it was hard to find a deck that didn't play four.

Diamond & Pearl /Platinum (2007–2009)

It was an era that produced grindy and skill-based formats, particularly since you could no longer claim prize cards as quickly with the removal of Pokémon-ex. Level X and SP Pokémon were the new gimmicks, and each of them were dominant forces in this era.

10. Luxray GL LV.X (Rising Rivals)

Gust effects have always been deadly in any format, but what made Luxray GL LV.X so good is it was a Pokémon-SP. This meant it benefited from all of the Team Galactic's Invention Trainer cards. Most notable of these was Energy Gain, which allowed it to attack for a single Lightning Energy, and Poké Turn, which allowed you to return Luxray to your hand and reuse its Bright Look Power.

8. Gardevoir (Secret Wonders)

Gardevoir had three things going for it that made it great. The first and most obvious was its Telepass Poké-Power, which allowed you a second Supporter each turn. The second was its Psychic Lock attack, which could be combined with hand disruption to further limit your opponent's options. And last, but not least, it evolved from the same line as the powerful Gallade, which could dish out one-hit KOs with its Psychic Cut attack (something Gardevoir rarely could do).

9. Garchomp C LV.X (Supreme Victors)

Garchomp C LV.X's true strength was released when Double Colorless Energy rejoined the format. This, combined with a handy Pokémon Tool called Energy Gain, allowed Garchomp to unleash its devastating Dragon Rush attack for a single Double Colorless Energy. You could deliver this attack on your opponent's benched Claydol to deny them access to its crucial Cosmic Power Poké-Power. From there, your opponent's board typically crumbled.

7. Broken Time-Space (Platinum)

It was originally Rare Candy that allowed Stage 2 Pokémon to keep up with speedier Basic and Stage 1 Pokémon, but Broken Time-Space was even better. That's because you could evolve unlimited Pokémon as early as the first turn of the game. Players used this card to achieve incredible Turn 1 setups, like a board full of card-drawing Claydols and an attacking Stage 2 Pokémon, such as Kingdra or Machamp.

6. Call Energy (Majestic Dawn)

It was as strong as it was unique. Call Energy allowed you to search out and bench two Basic Pokémon if it was attached to an Active Pokémon. This was particularly useful during the Diamond & Pearl era since players were not allowed to use any type of Trainer cards (including Supporters) on the first turn of the game.

3. Spiritomb (Arceus)

By the time Spiritomb debuted in the Arceus set, some really good Trainers (we've been talking about Trainers for 10 pages already, no need to explain) were taking over the format. Spiritomb's Keystone Seal put the brake on these powerful cards while simultaneously allowing you to set up with its 0-Energy Darkness Grace attack.

5. Cyrus's Conspiracy (Platinum)

The main reason Pokémon-SP were so powerful back in 2009 and 2010? Cyrus's Conspiracy. The card was often chained, fetching out another Cyrus's Conspiracy, with players grabbing one of four useful Team Galactic's Inventions each time they played it. These "Invention" Trainer cards allowed you to block your opponent's Poké-Powers, speed up your own attacks, fetch out Pokémon-SP from your deck, or return them from play to your hand. Talk about options!

2. Claydol (Great Encounters)

Perhaps the best card-drawing ability of all time, Claydol's Cosmic Power not only drew your hand up to six cards, but in a convenient way. It required you to put either one or two cards from your hand on the bottom of your deck before drawing, but this requirement worked in the user's benefit since you could stow away cards you didn't need and then draw more cards as a result.

4. Roseanne's Research (Secret Wonders)

Supporters that search out Basic Pokémon have always been good, but the fact that Roseanne's Research let you choose whatever split of Basic Energy and Basic Pokémon you wanted made it the era's best Supporter. Instead of being useless later in the game, Roseanne's Research continued to be useful by providing ways to find Basic Energy.

1. Uxie (Legends Awakened)

We're used to Pokémon with card-drawing Abilities today, but Uxie was the first of its kind when it debuted in the Legends Awakened set in 2008. Permitting explosive first turns, Uxie not only gave every deck a big consistency boost, but it could also be abused in multiples to create drawn-out, insane turns. These lengthy turns could even ultimately end with an attacking Stage 2 Pokémon thanks to Broken Time-Space.

HeartGold SoulSilver (2010-2011)

A short-lived era that placed an emphasis on Evolved Pokémon, the HS sets brought Pokémon Prime as well as the two-piece Pokémon-LEGEND into the game. Pokémon-LEGEND saw little competitive success, but Pokémon Prime dominated. The HS era also featured some of the greatest Supporters the game would ever see.

10. Magnezone Prime (Triumphant)

Magnezone was used primarily for its Magnetic Draw Poké-Power, but its Lost Burn attack could deliver huge attacks capable of one-hit KO'ing any Pokémon you encountered.

8. Cleffa (HeartGold SoulSilver, Call of Legends)

A throwback to the legendary Neo Genesis Cleffa, HeartGold SoulSilver's Cleffa drew one less card, but could attack for free. This meant you could pay a Pokémon's Retreat Cost on the first turn and still get a new hand. This was a big deal!

9. Typhlosion Prime (HeartGold SoulSilver)

Typhlosion's Firestarter allowed you to not just power up massive attacks, but also repeat them. Among these were Reshiram's 120-damage Blue Flare and even Rayqyaza & Deoxys-LEGEND's 150-damage Ozone Blaster.

7. Pokémon Communication

(HeartGold SoulSilver)

A convenient way to set up since it didn't use up your Supporter for the turn, Pokémon Communication was a reliable Item that fit into many different decks.

6. Rare Candy (Unleashed)

Rare Candy had already existed in past eras, and it's fair to say it was great in all of them. However, it earns a spot in the Top 10 in the HeartGold SoulSilver era simply because there were so many powerful Stage 2 Pokémon during this time period in the game.

3. Smeargle (Undaunted, Call of Legends)

Smeargle's Portrait allowed you a second—and if you had another one, even a third— Supporter on your turn. This produced ridiculous turns, like a Darkrai EX delivering a three-Energy Night Spear attack as early as the first turn of the game.

5. Yanmega Prime (Triumphant)

Yanmega's Insight allowed you to execute two solid attacks for no Energy. But what made Yanmega so good is that there were so many ways to match your opponent's hand size. You could play Copycat, for example, or use Magnezone's Magnetic Draw. If your hand got too large, you could reduce it with Junk Arm.

2. Junk Arm (Triumphant)

Just like the original Item Finder of Base Set, Junk Arm existed in a format with several very strong Trainer cards. The most notable of these was Pokémon Catcher. Thanks to Junk Arm, you could easily chain Pokémon Catchers, attacking your opponent's benched Pokémon turn after turn. It's no surprise that when these two cards existed together, the format was lightning-fast and reminiscent of the Haymaker days of 1999.

4. Twins (Triumphant)

Searching out any two cards from your deck is an incredibly powerful effect, but what was even stronger was the ability to chain this card turn after turn. You could use Twins to search out a useful card and then a second Twins, preparing for your next turn. If you weren't ready to reclaim the prize lead, you could repeat this as many as three times, accessing whatever you needed turn after turn.

1. Pokémon Collector

(HeartGold SoulSilver)

Over the years, there have been plenty of Supporters that have searched out two Basic Pokémon, but any time a Supporter allowed you to pick three, it usually came with some type of restriction. This wasn't the case with Pokémon Collector. One of the greatest Supporters of all time for early game setup, Pokémon Collector set players up for powerful second and third turns by getting them all the Basic Pokémon they needed.

Black & White
(2012–2013)

The Black & White era could best be summarized as the game returning to its roots, with Basic Pokémon again dominating in the form of high-HP Pokémon-EX. Decks that drew prizes quickly saw plenty of success, but that didn't mean some Evolution-based decks weren't winning either.

10. Dark Patch (Dark Explorers)

Initially it powered up strong Pokémon like Darkrai-EX, and in XY, it further increased the damage capability of Yveltal EX's Evil Ball attack. Dark Patch continued to be played in the Expanded format years after its release.

8. Tropical Beach (Black & White Promo)

Since Rare Candy could not be played on the first turn during the Black & White era, Evolution-based decks generally had nothing better to do but pass their first turn. What better card, then, than Tropical Beach? Tropical Beach allowed you to end your turn with a solid 7 cards, setting you up for an impressive second turn.

9. Jirachi EX (Plasma Blast)

Is there anything worse than an opening hand with no Supporters? Jirachi EX's Stellar Guidance was insurance against this predicament, allowing every Ultra Ball and Level Ball to double as a way to get you a Supporter. Not only could Jirachi EX bail you out of a pinch, but it let you choose which Supporter, so you could also use it to find the perfect Supporter later in the game.

7. Hypnotoxic Laser (Plasma Storm)

As if the automatic Poison wasn't good enough, Hypnotoxic Laser also had a 50% chance of leaving your opponent's Active Pokémon Asleep. On top of that, you could boost this Poison damage to 3 damage counters with Virbank City Gym. This combination of Hypnotoxic Laser & Virbank City Gym was used in a variety of aggressive decks, delivering knockouts on your opponent's Pokémon before they could even finish setting up.

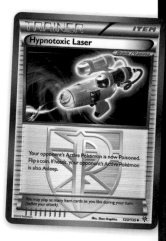

6. Keldeo EX (Boundaries Crossed)

Keldeo EX was a great partner for Blastoise, since Blastoise could use its Deluge Ability to flood Keldeo EX with Water Energy to produce a massive Secret Sword attack. But Keldeo EX was a versatile Pokémon that was used more for its Rush In ability than its attack. Given that it existed in a format where Special Conditions were prevalent, Rush In was a useful way to escape these. You could then use a variety of tricks (the most popular being Float Stone) to easily bring Keldeo EX back to safety on the Bench.

5. Sableye (Dark Explorers)

Sableye's strength was derived from its Junk Hunt attack, allowing players to easily recover Item cards they had already used or been forced to discard with Professor Juniper. As more powerful Item cards were released, like Puzzle of Time and VS Seeker, Sableye's Junk Hunt only grew stronger.

4. Professor Juniper (Black & White, Dark Explorers, Plasma Blast)

A fresh hand of 7 cards will always be powerful in the Pokémon TCG, just as it was during the Base Set days in the form of Professor Oak. But Professor Juniper was particularly strong during the Black & White era because there was not yet a restriction on attacking if you played first. The quick pressure enabled by drawing this new hand generally outweighed the cost of discarding a few cards.

3. N (Noble Victories, Dark Explorers)

Just like Rocket's Admin. that preceded it, N was great both early and late in the game. In the first few turns, it provided a fresh hand of 6 cards, and late in the game, you could hit your opponent down to 1 card—the ultimate form of disruption. N stole countless games from opponents who were so close to victory!

2. Pokémon Catcher (Emerging Powers, Dark Explorers, Plasma Blast)

Before it received an errata requiring a coin flip, Pokémon Catcher was a force to be reckoned with. This card, combined with the fact that there was not yet a restriction on attacking if you played first, allowed aggressive strategies to thrive. You could ruin an opponent's day with a series of Pokémon Catchers, knocking out their weak Pokémon before they could set up. Alternatively, you could use it to claim your final two prize cards by bringing a weak Pokémon-EX into the Active spot to knock out.

1. Ultra Ball (Dark Explorers, Plasma Freeze, Plasma Blast)

So simple, yet so effective. The strength of Ultra Ball stems from the fact that it was an Item card, not a Supporter. In the past, the best Pokémon-fetching Trainer were generally Supporter cards, but Ultra Ball could be played the same turn as your Supporter, allowing you to do more in one turn than you were accustomed to.

XY
(2014–2016)

XY brought the short-lived Fairy type into the TCG and can best be summarized as the beginning of modern Pokémon, where players have access to huge amounts of cards each turn thanks to easily-accessible card-drawing Abilities. With turns sometimes lasting 5+ minutes, players could produce incredible setups after only one turn.

10. Trevenant (XY)

Being able to lock your opponent out of Item cards as early as the second turn was already solid, but Trevenant only became stronger when it gained Wally, which allowed a Turn 1 Trevenant, and then even stronger again when Trevenant BREAK was released.

8. Muscle Band (XY)

+20 damage and no restrictions? Wow! Muscle Band allowed massive attacks like Yveltal EX's Evil Ball to reach even higher amounts of damage—enough to one-hit KO other Pokémon-EX. It also allowed attacks like Seimitoad EX's 30-damage Quaking Punch to be more effective, since the low damage output of these attacks would sometimes give your opponent too much time otherwise.

9. Double Colorless Energy (XY, Phantom Forces, Generations, Fates Collide, Evolutions)

Double Colorless Energy sped up and boosted several already solid attacks. Yveltal EX's Evil Ball got a +40 damage boost from it, while Seismitoad EX could deliver its devastating Quaking Punch for a single Energy card. It also allowed Shaymin EX to return itself to the user's hand with Sky Return, which was great to both reuse its Set Up Ability or deny your opponent an easy two-Prize target.

7. VS Seeker (Phantom Forces, Roaring Skies)

The XY era was filled with a variety of Supporters, so you can think of VS Seeker almost like a wild card that gave you a lot of options. This allowed skilled players to carefully select the best Support each turn and outplay their opponent. It wasn't just skillful, but fun too!

6. Seismitoad EX (Furious Fists)

Seismitoad EX's Quaking Punch could be delivered turn after turn, denying your opponent access to critical Item cards. But the most annoying part of playing against Seismitoad EX was its beefy 180 HP. It took a lot of effort to knock out a 180 HP Pokémon without access to Item cards, and by the time you finally did, your opponent might already have two more powered up to attack you with!

5. Yveltal EX (XY)

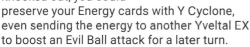

Both of Yveltal EX's attacks were good, but the main driver behind Yveltal EX's success was Evil Ball. With so many different ways to boost Evil Ball's damage (Double Colorless Energy, Muscle Band, Dark Patch, Hypnotoxic Laser), the attack could take down even the highest HP Pokémon. When Yveltal EX was in danger of being knocked out, you could preserve your Energy cards with Y Cyclone, even sending the energy to another Yveltal EX to boost an Evil Ball attack for a later turn.

4. N (Fates Collide)

Sick of reading about how good N was? Well, that's because it was that good. Like the Black & White era, the XY era was dominated by Pokémon-EX. As soon as your opponent took a knockout against one, they claimed two Prizes, which meant N was delivering them two less cards.

3. Forest of Giant Plants (Ancient Origins)

Forest of Giant Plants enabled two of the most frustrating elements ever to play against. The first was Vileplume, an Item-blocking Stage 2 that could enter play on the first turn. Even worse, though? In the Expanded format, Shiftry from the Next Destinies set gained a way to enter play first turn thanks to a Grass-type Seedot & Nuzleaf. This Shiftry could return an opponent's Pokémon to their hand, meaning multiple Shiftry could easily defeat a player on the first turn. It was so out of control Shiftry had to be banned!

2. Ultra Ball (Flashfire, Roaring Skies, Fates Collide)

Just as it was in the Black & White era, Ultra Ball remained the best Item card in the XY years that followed. It continued to supplement Supporters, allowing players to do more in a single turn than a lone Supporter would. Since it could be used to search out Shaymin EX, this meant any Ultra Ball doubled as a source of draw.

1. Shaymin EX (Roaring Skies)

Shaymin EX's Set Up drew 1 less card than Uxie's Set Up in the Diamond & Pearl era, but Shaymin EX was an even better card. Why? Because Shaymin EX existed in the same format as Ultra Ball. This meant players had easy access to Shaymin EX and the games could begin with an immediate (and lengthy) turn of multiple Set Up Abilities. The result of this card was pure insanity; it completely changed the way the game was played.

Sun & Moon
(2017–2019)

With the introduction of GX-Pokémon, the game saw a new mechanic in GX-attacks. These attacks were incredibly powerful but could only be used once in a game. How players timed these attacks could often be game deciding, similar to the Z-move mechanic in the video games. Tag-Team GX Pokémon was also released as the game's first three prize Pokémon, which made games faster than ever before.

10. Jirachi

Jirachi makes a return as one of the best Support Pokémon in the game with its Stellar Wish Ability, allowing the player to pick any Trainer card from the top 5 cards of their deck. By using switching effects, the player could even use multiple Stellar Wish every turn throughout the game.

8. Reset Stamp

Previously printed as a similar effect on supporter cards like Rocket's Admin and N, Reset Stamp is just a one-way disruption method in form of an item. This is usually a much stronger effect than N in the later stages of the game, when both players have taken multiple prize cards, but in the early game it is at the same time less useful.

9. Oranguru

Resource Management could put any 3 cards from the discard pile back into the deck, making it an incredible Pokémon for control and stall decks that tried to win on resources rather than prize cards. At the same time, it would also be one of the best possible options to use against this sort of strategy as well, making sure you would not deck out.

7. Mewtwo & Mew GX

Its Ability Perfection allowed Mewtwo & Mew GX to copy any attacks of GX Pokémon in the discard pile. This meant that players could launch powerful attacks from all kinds of Pokémon, even stage 1 and stage 2 Pokémon, with much less effort than before. Flexibility was a huge part of this card's success, since the same Pokémon was able to threaten so many different attacks at once.

6. Pikachu & Zekrom GX

Probably the strongest competitive card featuring Pokémon's main mascot Pikachu in the TCG. Full Blitz dealt an impressive amount of damage, while simultaneously charging up a backup attacker or itself to prepare for the full effect of Tag Bolt GX on the following turn.

3. Tapu Lele GX

The Wonder Tag Ability lets the player grab any supporter card from the deck when Tapu Lele GX enters the bench, making it an excellent support Pokémon for any deck. Although it's not the first time we had this Ability on a Pokémon, Tapu Lele GX also proved useful as an attacker with its Energy Drive attack and by having no weakness.

5. Garbodor

Trashalanche was a great way to keep fast decks in check, by doing 20 times the amount of Item cards in the opponents discard pile. Players often had to consider how many items they could afford to run when building their decks to not get overly punished by Garbodor.

2. Arceus & Dialga & Palkia GX

One of the most infamous cards of all time thanks to its Altered Creation GX attack. For the rest of the game the player would draw an extra prize card for each knockout, and even do 30 more damage with all attacks. This pushed single prize strategies almost completely out of the format, as they would have a hard time competing when giving up an additional prize card.

4. Guzma

Talking about effects that targets opposing benched Pokémon and puts them in the active position, Guzma was probably the pinnacle as far as Supporters goes. Not only could it target any benched Pokémon, but it gave the player a way to switch out their own active Pokémon as well. This was huge for deck building, meaning players could often save space by playing fewer switching cards in general.

1. Zoroark GX

Few cards have ever seen as much competitive success as Zoroark GX. With its Trade Ability it allowed players to draw through their deck quickly, while discarding less needed cards along the way. Its Riotous Beating attack could be fueled by a single Double Colorless Energy, making it an efficient attacker as well.

Sword & Shield
(2020-2022)

In this era, V and VMAX Pokémon made its debut. V Pokémon were powerful Pokémon worth 2 prize cards that also could evolve into an even more powerful form in VMAX, which like the Tag-Team GX Pokémon also were worth 3 prize cards to knock out. Sword & Shield later gave us VSTAR Pokémon with V-Star Powers. Just like GX-attacks, these could only be used once a game, but this time powerful V-Star Abilities were also an option, in addition to V-Star attacks.

10. Rapid Strike Urshifu VMAX

Rapid Strike Urshifu VMAX is a perfectly balanced card with a cost-effective attack in Gale Trust, and a versatile attack in G-Max Rapid Flow. Being able to threaten a 2-hit KO on a big active Pokémon also having the option to knock out weaker targets on the bench makes Rapid Strike Urshifu VMAX a scary Pokémon to play against for most decks.

8. Archeops

Fossil Pokémon have traditionally been very difficult to use because of the many clunky mechanics to get them into play. Thanks to Lugia VSTAR, Archaeops' incredible Ability gets a chance to shine. The Primal Turbo Ability lets the player attach any 2 special energies from their deck onto any Pokémon in play. This is used to charge Pokémon that would normally be very difficult to use and unleash powerful attacks to overwhelm the opponent.

9. Comfey

With its Flower Selecting Ability, Comfey is the key component in all decks that use cards that revolve around the Lost Zone. By utilizing Scoop Up Net and switching between multiple Comfey a turn, players can quickly draw through their deck, while also getting cards in the Lost Zone to activate their most powerful cards.

7. Genesect V

Fusion Strike System is a draw power unlike anything we have seen in the game before. With a full field of Fusion Strike Pokémon, the player could potentially draw until they have six cards in their hand up to four times every single turn. Genesect V is used as the main engine of the Mew VMAX archetype, which includes other powerful cards such as Power Tablet.

6. Zacian V

Pokémon that draw cards have always been strong, and so is the case for Zacian V. Intrepid Sword not only draws three cards from the deck, but can also help charge Zacian V by attaching any metal energy found among those cards. Brave Blade is a strong attack for a Basic Pokémon, which made Zacian V an essential part of multiple top tier decks.

3. Scoop Up Net

The powerful effect of returning a Pokémon from play to your hand usually has a major downside, like being reliant on a coin flip, or even spending your supporter for the turn. Granted, Scoop Up Net does not work on Pokémon V or Pokémon GX, but it still comes with a lot of great uses, which include retreating, healing and reusing Abilities. Some of the cards on this list would not be nearly as good without Scoop Up Net.

5. Arceus VSTAR

The god of all Pokémon has it all: high HP, a high damage attack with energy acceleration, and great support for its colorless typing. With an Ability to pick up any 2 cards from the deck on top of that, Arceus VSTAR can pair well with almost any type of V Pokémon in the format, and has with its versatility won a ton of events since its printing in Brilliant Stars.

2. Marnie

Marnie can be used regardless of prizes taken, which makes it one of the best disruption cards available in the early stages of the game. It creates a slight card advantage for the player using the card as well, and ensures in general more useful draws than a regular shuffle-draw supporter since the cards are sent to the bottom of the deck.

4. Radiant Greninja

Radiant cards are limited to a single copy in your deck, but Radiant Greninja grants the player the Ability to cycle through their energy cards with ease. Moonlight Shuriken is also a great attack to target weaker support Pokémon. With all the cards that can interact with energy cards in the discard pile, this card will be a natural inclusion in a variety of decks, even those without water energy.

1. Inteleon

The Shady Dealings Ability gave us arguably the strongest engine of all time. Picking up any two trainer cards when evolving usually translates to any two cards, since a lot of trainer cards can search out both Pokémon and Energy. Scoop Up Net and Drizzile with almost the same Ability makes this especially powerful.

Should You Get Your Pokémon Cards Graded?

By Bill Gill

During the summer of 2020, "graded Pokémon" cards were one of the hottest collectibles in the world. Prices skyrocketed! A PSA 10 graded Charizard card sold for $369,000 in 2020! The growing demand for card grading services went bonkers. PSA, the gold standard in card grading, raised their service prices and then suspended its services for a while just to catch up. New card grading services jumped into the market as well. It was pretty much chaos in 2020 and 2021 – prices climbed, and it was nearly impossible to get any Pokémon cards graded anywhere.

Well, it is 2023, and the Pokémon card market has come down a bit from the record highs of 2020, but many graded Pokémon cards are still extremely valuable, and all the grading companies have caught up on their backlogs. Is it still worth getting some of your Pokémon cards professionally graded?

What are Graded Cards?

A *graded card* is a trading card that has been sent to a professional grading company and assigned a quality rating. The grading companies have teams of Professional Graders who grade sports cards and other collectible cards. The cards are graded on a scale from 1 to 10.

The Basic Grading Scale:

10: Gem Mint
9: Mint
8: Near Mint-Mint
7: Near Mint
6: Excellent- Mint

5: Excellent
4: Very Good – Excellent
3: Very Good
2: Good
1: Poor

Half point grades are possible. For example, a 1.5 would be fair.

After the cards have been graded by the professional grading company, the cards are given unique certification identification numbers, entered into a database, carefully sealed in custom tamper-evident holders (encapsulated), and returned to their owners.

So, Why Have Pokémon Cards Graded?

First: Graded cards can sell for a lot more than ungraded cards! If you want to buy a mint First Edition Charizard on eBay, you have two choices. You can either buy an ungraded card, and trust the seller when he says the card is mint. Or you can buy a graded, sealed card and know the card is truly mint. Some buyers will take a chance on ungraded, while others will pay more to get exactly what they want. A PSA Graded Gem Mint "10" Skyridge Secret Rare Holo Crystal Charizard sold for $15,000 on eBay in December 2022. The highest sale price we could find on an ungraded version of that same Charizard card was $2000.

Second: The encapsulation itself is actually fantastic and it protects the card from future damage. There are several ways to protect your cards at home, but none are foolproof. Encapsulation is one of the better ways to protect your most valuable cards.

Pojo Note: Many people call these encapsulations "slabs".

What are the Card Grading Services?

There are now three big players out there for grading cards:

PSA
(Professional Sports Authenticator)

BGS
(Beckett Grading Service)

CGC
(Certified Guarantee Company)

PSA is the most popular with Pokémon collectors, but the other companies are excellent as well. I have used them all, and I like them all.

How Much Does It Cost to have a Pokémon Card Graded?

- PSA charges about $19/card. Cards must have a declared value of $499 or less. (If your cards are worth more, it will cost you more to grade your cards.)
- CGC charges about $15/card. Cards must have a declared value of $250 or less.
- BGS charges about $25/card. Cards worth more than $100 will be affected with more shipping and insurance charges.

A thing to remember is that you have to pay for shipping & insurance both ways, so those prices are just a starting point. Prices can do go down with some grading companies if you send cards in bulk, and sometimes there might be reduced rates and monthly specials for members.

Should You Get Your Pokémon Cards Graded?

This is a tough question to answer. Usually it does not make sense to have a card graded unless it is very old and/or in Near Mint Condition. We would say if a card is very collectable card, and worth over $100 "ungraded", you might want to consider getting it graded. We also recommend you only submit cards for grading if you think they will receive scores of 8, 9 or a 10. If a card is extremely rare, and/or extremely collectible, then it might be worth sending in lower grade copies.

Check the Completed Sales section on eBay and find the prices that cards have actually sold for, not what they are listed at. First-Edition, Base Set Holographic Pokémon Cards sell at great prices, as do "chase" cards from many of the sets.

Prepare to be Disappointed with Your Grades!

It is really difficult to get cards graded at a 9 or a 10, especially on older cards. Cards need to be centered perfectly. They have to be cut perfectly. They can't have dings to the corners, or white edges, or surface scratches. There can be no roughness on the face or edges. For Pokémon cards, look closely at the holofoil artwork for any scratches. Turn the card over, and look for any whiteness around the blue edges.

Many older cards you might thought were perfect can come back as 7's or 8's. Ten's basically have to be protected from the get-go … taken directly from a booster pack and highly protected immediately. And then they still would have to be centered perfectly, and not have any damage that could have occurred before and after you opened them.

Here are 20 recent sales (from December 2022) of graded Pokémon cards from eBay and other Auction Houses:

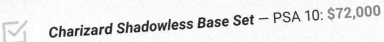

- ☑ Charizard Shadowless Base Set — PSA 10: **$72,000**
- ☑ Charizard 1st Edition Base Set — PSA 8: **$9,600**
- ☑ Charizard 1st Edition Base Set — CGC 8: **$9,500**
- ☑ Charizard Expedition — PSA 10: **$8,100**
- ☑ Skarmory Expedition Holo — PSA 10: **$15,000**
- ☑ Umbreon Gold Star Pop Series 5 — PSA 10: **$14,000**
- ☑ Lt. Surge's Electabuzz Gym Heroes 1st Edition Holo — CGC 10: **$8,000**
- ☑ 1st Edition Red Cheeks Pikachu Pokémon Base Set — PSA 10: **$5,200**
- ☑ Shining Mewtwo Neo Destiny — PSA 10: **$5,000**
- ☑ Shining Charizard Neo Destiny — BGS 9.5: **$5,000**
- ☑ Charizard Unlimited Neo Destiny — PSA 10: **$3,600**
- ☑ Lugia Neo Genesis Unlimited Holo — CGC 9.5: **$3,000**
- ☑ Mudkip Gold Star Team Rocket Returns Holo — PSA 9: **$1,900**
- ☑ Blastoise 1st Edition Base Set — PSA 8: **$1,800**
- ☑ Pikachu Poké Card Creator Contest WB Kids Promo — PSA 8: **$700**
- ☑ Mudkip Kids' WB Poké Card Creator Promo — PSA 9: **$420**
- ☑ Pikachu Vmax Vivid Voltage — PSA 10: **$450**
- ☑ Dark Charizard 1st Edition Team Rocket Holo Rare — CGC 8: **$340**
- ☑ Charizard V Full Art Champions Path — PSA 10: **$340**
- ☑ Mew Prime HGSS Triumphant Holo — CGC 9.5: **$190**

Still Pokémon Go-ing Strong

By Matthew Buck

Hello to all Pokémon Trainers!! You are probably aware of Pokémon Go and the soaring start it had when launched in 2016. The game had trainers of all ages running from town to town to catch all 151 original Pokémon. Now we find ourselves in 2023 (at the time of this article) and the game may not have the initial buzz it once had, but it seems to be stronger than ever!

Niantic and the Pokémon team have greatly expanded the Pokédex, improved trainer battle systems and functions, and even added featured and limited time events! Do not worry though because they have kept the core idea of the game at heart. The true soul of the game is still allowing every participant to live out their dream of being the Pokémon trainer they always wanted to be.

If you are a new trainer to the game, picking the game back up after a few years away, or looking to improve some tactics, the core game mechanics are still the same. We recommend reading *Pojo's Unofficial Ultimate Guide to Pokémon Go* to learn or refresh your knowledge of these mechanics. We wrote that book back in 2016 to help out new trainers and the advice can still help out trainers of all levels to this day.

Let us dive into some of the newer features so you can take advantage of everything Pokémon Go has to offer.

① Become a Battle-Hardened Hero

The core of every Pokémon game is leveling up your Pokémon and battling all the way to the top. Pokémon Go is no different from any other game in the franchise. If you click the little Pokéball in the center of your screen, you can select the option to join battles! In this battle mode, you will take on other real-life trainers in your local area in a 3-Vs-3 Pokémon duel. The first person to faint all of the other trainers' Pokémon wins. By following the prompt on the screen, you join a battle and select the battle league in which you want to duel.

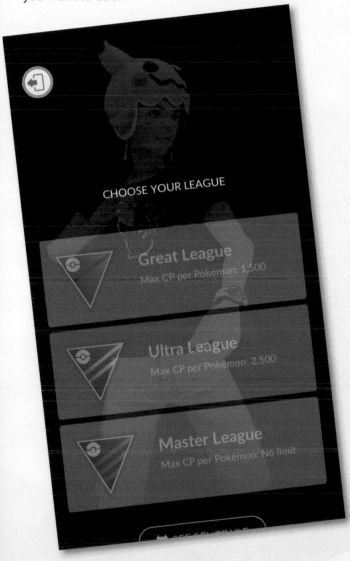

When picking a league, keep in mind your Pokémon's CP (CP is the Combat Power strength of each Pokémon and determines how well they will hold up in a fight). The lowest league is the Great League and allows all Pokémon up to CP level 1,500. Next is the Ultra League, which allows all Pokémon up to CP Level 2,500. The last is the Master League, which has no limit to the CP ranking. Be mindful because you do not want a CP 900 Bulbasaur going up against a CP 2,900 Charizard!!

These battles also take matchup type and attack or defense buffs into mind. The more wins you rack up in a league, the better rewards you will receive for winning battles. So, level up your Pokémon wisely and see who makes the cut for your ultimate battle squad.

② Did we Just Become Best Friends?

Every trainer has their own style of play. Some have their favorite Pokémon from day one and grow a bond stronger than Ash and his Pikachu. Others love to make new friends and go on adventures together while trying to "catch them all". We think it is best to have a mix of strategies, and Pokémon Go allows for you to forge your own playstyle.

The game offers a new feature called "Bonding" or "Friendship" levels. The first is a bonding level with your Pokémon. If you click on your trainer home button on the left side of the screen, you can select a Pokémon to be your buddy. You can then gain levels by feeding your Pokémon treats, taking pictures with them, petting them, and of course battling with your buddy. Doing all these activities earns you buddy points, and the more you earn the better rewards you get. Some rewards include: your buddy Pokémon becomes stronger and gives you bonuses in battles, your buddy can earn candy to help level up faster, and your buddy can help retrieve gifts from local Pokéstops.

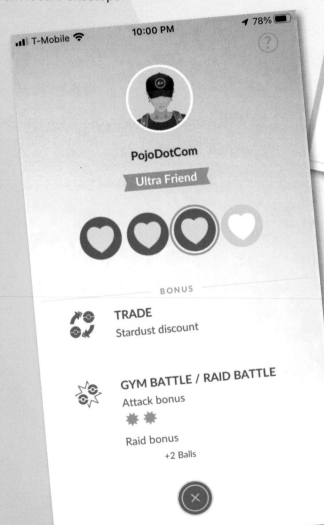

You may even get lucky and make your buddy so happy that they will burst out of their Pokéball and follow you around for a while. Do not worry about picking the correct buddy. Once you pick one you are not stuck with them. You can swap buddy Pokémon at any time without any penalty.

There is a similar system for the real-life friends you make in the game. You can see your friends in the same menu as the trainer profile. You can earn buddy points by battling in raids together, trading Pokémon and even sending gifts to each other. Just like Buddy Pokémon, the more you level up a friend, the better rewards you receive. With higher level friends, you can get boosts when you battle in raids and gyms together, get more items in a sent gift, and even increased chances to get Lucky Pokémon in trades.

3 Raid! Raid! Raid!

Have you ever been walking down the street and all of a sudden, a Legendary Pokémon is blocking the road?!? Of course not!! Legendary and Rare Pokémon earn those titles because they are hard to find. Pokémon Go has made it so Pokémon of this magnitude are also hard to find and not everyone can find one every day. The game does this by having raids at Pokémon Gyms in your area.

Every once in a while, at random times during the day, a gym transforms into a raid where special Pokémon can be battled and caught. Even though raids are random, you can track any ongoing raids by selecting the local Pokémon tracker on the lower right side of the screen and selecting the Raid tab. The Pokémon in raids range from 1-star battles to 5-star battles. 1-star battles are usually fun Event Pokémon like a Pikachu with a fun hat or starter Pokémon from the different generations. 3-star Pokémon usually are rare Pokémon that are very strong or not usually found in your geographical location. 5-star Pokémon are usually the Legendary fights reserved for Mewtwo, Groudon, Ho-Oh and others.

Anybody can join a raid if they are at the gym the raid took over. One good thing to come out of the pandemic were remote raid passes. With these special passes, you can join raids in your area without being at the gym and even invite friends that may be nowhere near the gym or even near you! 1- or 2-star raids can easily be done by yourself. 3-star raids can sometimes be done alone by high level trainers but are usually easy with a friend or two. 4- and 5-star raids can only be beaten in groups, as even the mightiest of trainers cannot take down such powerful Pokémon alone. The larger the group, the easier it will be to defeat the Pokémon.

You win a raid by battling the featured Pokémon like you would opposing Pokémon in a gym. However, if you defeat the Pokémon before time runs out, you will receive an opportunity to catch them. Just make sure to save your high-level berries for this occasion because you only get limited number of Safari balls to catch them.

4 (Zu)Batman: Justice for Pallet Town!

No Pokémon game would be complete without the presence of a Pokémon crime syndicate looking to wreak havoc on Pokémon players. Pokémon Go is plagued by the dastardly Team Rocket! Team Rocket Grunts will inhabit random local Pokéstops and harass nearby trainers. You can battle them to run them out of town and be the local hero. Battling any Team Rocket member gives you similar rewards to battling trainers. However, after a Team Rocket battle, you get a chance to catch and save one of the Pokémon they have brainwashed.

These "cursed" or shadow Pokémon usually have lower attack stats but extra strong defense stats alongside a lowered CP rating. Once you catch one of these Pokémon, you can keep them shadowed and level them up with the boosted defense, or you have the option to purify the Pokémon. Purifying a shadow Pokémon will increase their CP and give them an attack boost, but also lower their defense.

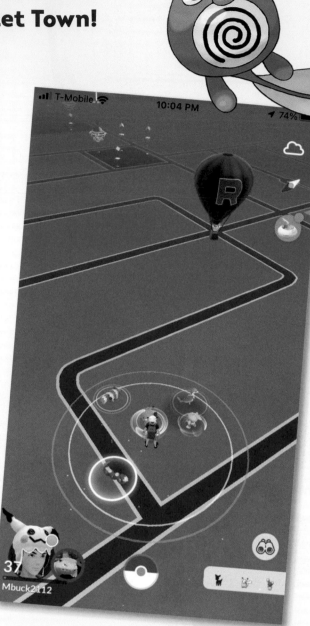

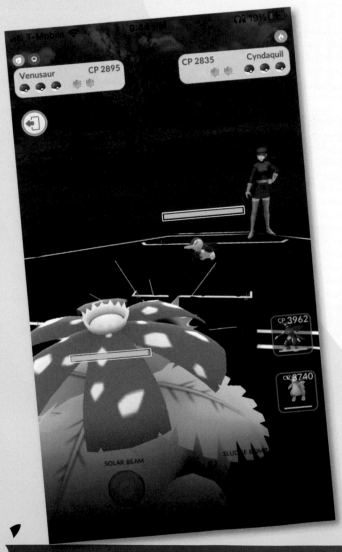

The most important thing a Team Rocket Grunt gives you is a piece of the Team Rocket Radar! By collecting 6 of these pieces, you will repair a full radar, which allows you to track down and battle Team Rocket leaders. These leaders are stronger than the Grunts, but also give you higher rewards and "cursed" Pokémon.

After eliminating enough leaders, the Team Rocket Boss Giovanni will appear to try to put an end to the disruption to his organized crime. Defeating Giovanni offers the best rewards for fighting Team Rocket. Also keep an eye out for special events that allow you to battle the devious dynamic duo - Jessie and James! Only you can keep your local streets safe!

PojoDotCom

sign

CP 54148

Mewtwo

0:59:03

▲0   BATTLE

PRIVATE GROUP

⑤ Featured Events and Items

We all love being a TM jockey and being able to change your Pokémon's attacks at will. However, certain items in the game can be harder to come by. You can collect these items by doing special missions and featured events. By clicking the binoculars button in the bottom right of your screen, it will pull up all the options for these missions.

Daily Missions usually refresh daily and offer quick rewards. Field Missions are ongoing "easy" missions. Completing at least one mission a day for 7 days can reward you with a bonus package that refreshes every time you earn it. Do not worry about missing a day, as progress continues where you left off.

Special missions are featured events that take longer to achieve but give you the best items and Pokémon. We highly recommend completing these missions because they not only make your adventures more fun, but they also give great rewards to boost your Pokémon and trainer level.

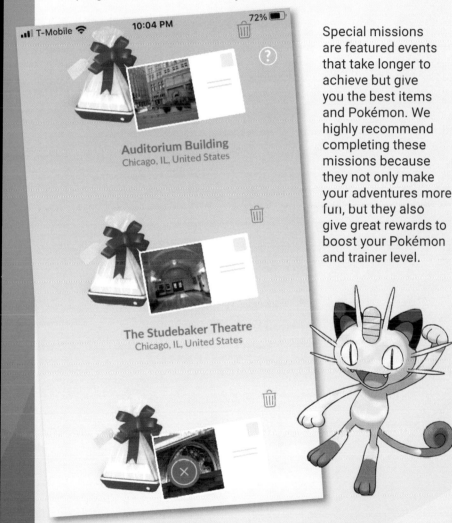

Always remember that there is not a "best way" to play Pokémon Go. The game offers many paths for you to take. You can carve out any path you want in the Pokémon world to help live out your dreams of being the trainer you always wanted to be.

Happy hunting!

Pokémon Video Games

Top 10 Pokémon of Each Type

By Angel Pelaez

Top 10 Pokémon
BY TYPE

After more than 25 years of Pokémon memories and incredible battles, I was asked to rank the **Top 10 Pokémon** for each of the 18 types there are. It took a great bit of testing and researching, and now I am quite confident in this list. This list should help you assemble a great team with your favorite Pokémon considering their strengths and weaknesses.

The competitive Pokémon game is an ever-evolving one (see what I did there?), so this list was assembled with certain considerations to keep in mind. The recent introduction of a new generation of Pokémon and new mechanics have changed the game recently and we are still experimenting on the potential of each Pokémon.

These days, Pokémon is a more complex game than the one we were playing back in the 90s. There are currently 1,008 known Pokémon across nine generations of videogames. So how should I choose just 180 of them? With the recent launch of Pokémon Scarlet & Violet, I had to decide on a few key points for this list that you should definitely keep in mind:

- All of these Pokémon are available to catch and/or get on Pokémon Scarlet and Violet at the time of writing (January 2023). More Pokémon are coming when Pokémon Home and Pokémon Go get updated and become compatible this Spring, but there is no sure way to know what Pokémon we're getting.

- Two exceptions to what I just wrote above are Cinderace and Charizard. I am including both in the lists because they have been introduced into the game via 7-star Raid Battles. More are confirmed to come.

- Some mechanics like Mega Evolution or Gigantamaxing are not present in the current version of Scarlet and Violet, so I am not talking about those mechanics very much.

- The order of Types and Pokémon are alphabetical and I am not ranking them from best to worst. But I do hope you find this order to be practical and easy to navigate.

- Terastallizing is the most recent and interesting mechanic in the new games, so I will be mentioning a suggested Tera Type for each Pokémon. But you can choose your favorite instead!

- Due to space limitations, I am not talking about suggested items or best natures for each Pokémon this time. There are many possibilities and complexities with this. I could write a whole book just on items and natures for all these Pokemon. ;-)

I would like to remind you there are now two ways you can get version-exclusive Pokémon if you're playing Scarlet or Violet: the traditional offline or online trade, and the new Union Circle which allows you to play with up to 4 players on their own version of Paldea. If the host has Scarlet and you are on Violet, you can explore and capture their version exclusives yourself, which makes completing the Pokédex a lot more fun.

You can also hone your skills battling online and learning from pro players on the many online resources we have now. The community is very friendly and we love sharing tips with each other. So don't be shy or get discouraged, and keep on battling!

Forretress

This Pokémon has had its fair share of popularity in past generations and still shines pretty well today. An Impish one with boosted defense stats will make for a very sturdy Pokémon capable of learning powerful moves such as Explosion, Double-Edge, Bug Buzz and Flash Cannon. A counter Tera Type such as water can also fight off his 4x weakness to Fire types!

Heracross

Having one of these with the Moxie hidden ability will allow you to have a very powerful Pokemon, even if it can't Mega-Evolve right now. A Steel Tera Type can make this an even stronger Pokemon.

Lokix

This Pokémon has a fantastic design and deserves some love for its great type combination. It's not the most powerful one, but an Adamant nature and Dark or Bug Tera Type will boost great moves such as Dark Pulse to a decent level.

Masquerain

A Modest nature on this one goes a long way with moves such as Air Slash or Hyper Beam. And a fighting Tera Type will surprise those rock type Pokémon that may be used as counters.

Rabsca

This is one very fun Pokémon to evolve, and I have enjoyed using it. Sure, it's not a Legendary but powerful moves like Bug Buzz and Gunk Shot have caught many by surprise when facing this Pokémon. Tera Type is flexible for this one too, so make it your own.

Scyther

Glad to see one of the OGs in this list! Scyther has never really needed to evolve to show off how strong it is. Scyther has access to moves like Aerial Ace and X-Scissor. Its main weakness to rock types can now be solved by having a fighting or steel Tera Type!

Slither Wing

A Lonely-natured specimen is a force to fear, no doubt about it. It has access to powerful moves such as Brick Break and Hyper Beam, and an electric Tera Type covers many of its main weaknesses.

Venomoth

This one might be considered one of the weakest on this list, but be mindful of its speed. A Sludge Bomb or Tera Blast from a Terastallized (poison type) Pokemon hurts really bad.

Vespiquen

I really like the flexibility of this Pokémon when it comes to its abilities Pressure, Intimidate or Unnerve. All 3 of them are fantastic to match with your preferred strategy. Attack Order and Defense Order are great theme-moves, and you can also choose Aerial Ace and Bug Buzz. A rock Tera Type is suggested.

Volcarona

This is one of the best bug-type Pokémon to raise with a Modest nature. You can choose a ground or steel Tera Type to solve its 4x weakness to rock types and sweep with moves such as Fire Blast and Hurricane.

Cacturne
A fantastic Pokémon to use in double battles with sandstorm users thanks to its Sand Veil ability. It is also a great Dark type with powerful moves such as Sucker Punch and Dark Pulse at its disposal. A fire Tera Type also works amazingly against its main weakness: bug types.

Honchkrow
This can be a scary Pokémon to go against. With a dark Tera Type, the hidden ability Moxie (boosts the attack stat after knocking out any Pokémon), and access to boosting moves such as Nasty Plot, it can hit really hard.

Houndoom
This one can be the very definition of "annoying" if you let it play. It is a great Special Attacker but can also counter many strategies thanks to its great move pool and access to moves such as Taunt and Will-O-Wisp.

Hydreigon
One of the best dragons in Pokémon history is now even better thanks to the possibility of getting a Tera Type that will get rid of its 4x weakness to fairy types, such as Poison or Steel. Moves like Draco Meteor and Dark Pulse are amazing for this one but you can also try out something different like U-Turn.

Iron Jugulis
The first Paradox Pokémon of this list is also a heavy hitter. Has access to great moves like Air Slash and Earth Power. The Quark Drive ability makes this a very popular choice for battles and Tera Raids and can be boosted even further with a dark Tera Type.

Mabosstiff
One of the "goodest boys" in Scarlet and Violet. This one is really special because of the access it has to a wide variety of move types - such as Crunch, Reversal, Play Rough and even Outrage - covering many weaknesses in your team. You can also be very flexible with its Tera Type.

Meowscarada
With access to the Protean hidden ability, Meowscarada is a very fast attacker capable of hitting hard and fast with utility moves such as U-Turn and Knock-Off. Flower Trick is also a fantastic move to have at your disposal if you're keeping the grass Tera Type.

Umbreon
This is a very disruptive and fun Pokémon to use thanks to a moveset that includes Fake Tears and Taunt. A psychic Tera Type can also take your opponents by surprise.

Weavile
This Pokémon hits hard and fast, and can boost its stats with moves such as Swords Dance. Choose between a dark Tera Type to boost your power even further or a fairy/psychic one to catch counters by surprise.

Zoroark
This has been a fan favorite for years thanks to its Illusion ability. It's a great option to open a battle and disrupt your opponent's strategy from the very first turn. Zoroark is also a great dark type offensive option with powerful moves such as Crunch and Knock Off at its disposal.

Appletun

Definitely one of my favorites from last generation, this one is the bulkiest choice, which is great to set up with Growth and attack with nice moves like Giga Drain or Dragon Pulse. A water, fire or steel Tera Type will counter ice types easily.

Baxcalibur

This generation's dragon did not disappoint at all. It's capable of boosting itself quite a lot thanks to moves like Swords Dance. Plus, it has some scary moves such as Icicle Crash and Glaive Rush. Be mindful of its type combination and solve its weaknesses with a counter Tera Type.

Cyclizar

Using this Pokémon is a lot of fun since it has access to a lot of move types that are both strong and surprising for your opponent: Dragon Claw, Acrobatics, Power Whip and Facade just to name a few. Boost your favorite moves with a matching Tera Type.

Dragapult

This one is just as strong now as it was in the past generation. It has an incredible movepool and an even scarier hidden ability (Cursed Body). A matching Dragon or Ghost Tera Type is recommended for further boosting.

Dragonite

This is still one of the best physical attackers out there and you will never regret training one of them. Moves like Extremespeed, Outrage and Fire Punch cover many weaknesses and you can match with a counter Tera Type to be on the safe side as well.

Flapple

Having access to grass types is always great given how many great competitive water types there are. And a dragon is always a good choice unless you're facing an ice type Pokémon. It has access to Grassy Terrain and Iron Defense to make it a bit bulkier and can cover weaknesses nicely with a fire or water Tera Type.

Garchomp

You already know that this is one great Pokémon, and despite losing Mega Evolution, it is still one of the best sweepers there are. The Swords Dance / Earthquake combo is even better when you choose a ground Tera Type, but you can choose a different one to counter the ice type weakness.

Goodra

This is another outstanding dragon type for many teams, although a more defensive one. Its hidden ability Gooey lowers your opponent's speed when it hits with a direct attack, so it is great to counter fast sweepers. It also has a great movepool including Rain Dance, Dragon Pulse, Sludge Bomb and Power Whip.

Haxorus

Yet another great sweeper joins the list, and this one gets better with interesting abilities such as Mold Breaker and Rivalry. It is capable of learning great moves such as Dragon Dance, Giga Impact and Crunch. Tera Type is flexible to cover any weaknesses.

Roaring Moon

This prehistoric Salamence loses the flying type in favor of the dark type, which makes it 4x weak to fairies but also makes it quite powerful. With moves like Outrage, Throat Chop and Earthquake, this will no doubt be one of the most loved Pokémon this generation.

Ampharos

This one did lose a bit of strength without Mega Evolution, but it is still one of my favorite Johto Pokémon to battle with. It has a great Special Attack, so try to take advantage of that with moves such as Electro Ball and Power Gem. A Tera Type will give it a bit more boost, but you can also choose something like Grass to cover its ground type weakness.

Bellibolt

This may not be the most powerful Electric type out there, but it's very popular thanks to Gym Leader Iono and it also honestly looks really cool. Hit smarter, not harder with this one using moves like Mud Shot, Muddy Water and Confuse Ray, and complement the strategy with a grass Tera Type.

Eelektross

This Pokémon can boost itself quite effectively thanks to moves such as Thunder Wave, Coil, and Electric Terrain. And it has some interesting moves that might catch your opponent by surprise like Flamethrower and Dragon Claw. Stay with an electric Tera Type to boost yourself further.

Electrode

This is still one of the fastest Pokémon out there, and quite dangerous too I might add. It can defend your team in double battles with moves such as Light Screen, but be mindful of its own weakness and choose a flying or water Tera Type that you can take advantage of with Tera Blast.

Jolteon

You already know this Pokemon looks cool, but it is also very fun to use - one of my favorite eeveelutions indeed. It is a straightforward Pokémon to use since you want to hit hard and switch with this one. Thunderbolt, Thunder Wave and Tera Blast are moves that go very well with an electric Tera Type.

Luxray

A great battle opponent thanks to the Intimidate ability, and also great to match with the Volt Switch move for a bit more freedom. But you can also make this a great utility Pokémon thanks to access to moves like Swagger and Thunder Wave.

Miraidon

Of course, you could expect one of the new Legendary Pokemon to be on this list. It has a great ability, and access to interesting moves that will allow you to use this one for battles or raids easily. I suggest Parabolic Charge, Dragon Pulse, Metal Sound and Electro Drift with an electric Tera Type.

Pawmot

I had a hard time figuring out how to evolve this one, but it was totally worth it. It is not the strongest electric type, but its fighting type gives you another counter route, and has a decent move pool that includes Close Combat, Revival Blessing and Giga Impact. Tera Type is flexible according to your preferences.

Rotom

This is still one of the most versatile Pokémon thanks to its unique ability to choose a second type according to your preference. Fan, Frist, Heat, Mow and Wash Rotom are all great so experiment with your favorite option and choose a Tera Type according to your needs. There are really a ton of options for this one!

Sandy Shocks

It was pretty weird encountering a ground type relative of Magnemite. But I have to admit this is one amazing Pokémon to train with a Modest nature and a flexible Tera Type according to your needs. For moves I suggest Thunderbolt, Flash Cannon, Earth Power and Volt Switch.

Dachsbun

Another "goodest boy" makes the list, and this is one great defensive option thanks in part to its ability Well-Baked Body. But I also like hitting hard with moves such as Double-Edge and Play Rough. Tera Type is also flexible, but try to choose one to counter your opponent's Pokémon.

Florges

This is not the most intimidating Pokémon, but it can become very powerful if you let it play out a strategy with moves such as Calm Mind, Grassy Terrain and Safeguard. It is also a great option for double battles. A poison, ground or rock Tera Type is recommended to cover its weaknesses.

Gardevoir

Having trouble against dragon types? This is one of the best counters there are and also a great doubles partner thanks to its Telepathy ability. It can also stand its ground with moves such as Draining Kiss, Misty Terrain and Disable. A matching Tera Type can boost its capabilities even further.

Grimmsnarl

This is one of those Pokémon that can sweep an entire team by themselves if you give it a few turns to set up moves like Bulk Up, Scary Face and Light Screen/Reflect. A fairy Tera Type is also great here.

Hatterene

One of my favs from Gen 8 and definitely a worthy fairy type to try out. It has access to great moves such as Dazzling Gleam, Psychic and Dark Pulse. It can also have a flexible Tera Type to cover weaknesses.

Mimikyu

Still a great option thanks to the free turn that its unique ability Disguise provides. You can use this turn to boost with moves such as Swords Dance, Curse or annoy with Will-O-Wisp, and then proceed to attack with Play Rough, Shadow Sneak or Shadow Claw. I really like this one with a ghost Tera Type.

Iron Valiant

This is one great support Pokémon thanks to its great stats and ability to set up defenses such as Reflect and Light Barrier. You can also disrupt other strategies with Taunt. It's great for double battles and raid battles as well. You can complement with a counter-oriented Tera Type as needed.

Scream Tail

Another great defensive Paradox Pokémon on the list that can become very dangerous, very fast. It can set up Stealth Rock, Thunder Wave and boost itself with Calm Mind as well. Tera Type for this one is also flexible.

Sylveon

Its Pixilate ability is great to stand its own ground since it can also boost a bit before attacking. You can start using Calm Mind and Fake Tears and complement with offensive moves such as Draining Kiss and Hyper Voice. Choose a Tera Type to counter poison or steel types.

Tinkaton

The fairy/steel type combo is kind of scary and provides great offensive and defensive possibilities. Set up Reflect and Swords Dance and then sweep away with powerful moves such as Gigaton Hammer and Play Rough. Of course, there are many other great move choices according to your needs. I recommend a water Tera type.

Armarouge

This is a great Pokémon for those who didn't choose the fire starter and it is great for the story, raid battles and even versus battles. It has many weaknesses but can make up for them with powerful moves like Armor Cannon, Psychic and Shadow Ball. Choose a Tera Type to cover weaknesses as you need.

Arcanine

Another OG that made it to the list and this one is still as great as it was back then! A pure fire-type with great stats and access to Intimidate is a great battle opener. It also has access to great moves such as Extreme Speed, Crunch and Fire Fang. Choose a Tera Type to counter any weaknesses you might encounter.

Camerupt

This Pokémon is kind of slow for the taste of many but it packs a punch that is worth checking out. It can set up games with moves like Yawn and Sunny Day, following up with others such as Earthquake and Fire Blast. A water Tera Type works nicely here.

Ceruledge

This is an excellent Pokémon to use in Tera Raids and battles thanks to a movepool that is both beneficial for itself and others. Bitter Blade and Swords Dance go amazingly well together, and moves like Taunt or Bulk Up are also great for a support role. Watch out for its many type weaknesses and choose a Tera Type accordingly.

Charizard

Who doesn't know how great Charizard is at this point? I'm really grateful it is here thanks to 7-star Tera Raids and it is still a force to be reckoned with. You can choose a fighting Tera Type and use powerful moves such as Focus Blast and Overheat and you'll have a blast!

Chi-Yu

This new legendary is scary thanks to the move Ruination which cuts HP in half. But if you don't like that route you can still choose among great moves such as Dark Pulse, Overheat and Tera Blast. Choose a Tera Type that covers one of its weaknesses, such as water or flying.

Cinderace

Another great addition to the Fire squad and one of the most beloved fire starters of the past few generations. Libero is still a decent ability to have and how can you not love moves like Pyro Ball or High Jump Kick. I recommend a flying Tera Type for this one, but this is flexible.

Flareon

Not the most popular of the Eeveelutions but still an amazing Pokémon. Also, pretty straightforward to use so it is great for new players. Just teach it Fire Fang, Trailblaze, Flare Blitz and Will-o-Wisp and you're good to go. I also recommend looking for a grass Tera Type.

Scovillain

I love this Pokémon's design! And it is also a pretty fun one to use with its Moody hidden ability. You can choose to boost fire or grass type moves with a matching Tera Type, boost a bit with Growth and then sweep with moves like Overheat or Leaf Storm.

Torkoal

Torkoal is a pretty defensive Pokémon with some great utilities for your team. You can open with one of these with the Drought ability and start using moves like Yawn, Clear Smog and Sunny Day to disrupt further. Choose a Tera Type to cover weaknesses as needed.

Annihilape

At last, a new Primeape evolution! And I wasn't disappointed at all. This is a great physical sweeper if you can survive long enough for it to boost with moves such as Bulk Up and then attack with powerful options like Rage Fist or Drain Punch. Choose the fighting or ghost Tera Type and go all out!

Breloom

Yet another excellent physical attacker also capable of some disruption thanks to its Effect Spore ability. Moves like Bullet Seed, Mach Punch and Bulldoze are amazing options. A rock Tera Type will keep you safe from its biggest weakness: flying type moves.

Crabominable

A Brave-natured one is something scary to face since it also has some great moves at its disposal such as Ice Hammer, Slam and Rock Smash. Since it is a slow Pokémon, you need to cover the weaknesses that come with this type combination with an appropriate Tera Type.

Gallade

This is one amazing sweeper with access to some great moves like Psycho Cut and Brick Break. But you can also train it differently as a utility Pokémon with moves such as Hypnosis, Psychic Terrain and Disable. Try to choose a Tera Type depending on what you're facing.

Great Tusk

There's a lot to love about Great Tusk, including powerful moves such as Earthquake, Giga Impact or Close Combat, as well as some others to boost survivability such as Taunt and Knock Off. It has a lot of weaknesses, so choose a Tera Type to counter properly.

Iron Hands

Definitely one of the most used Pokémon in raid battles right now, and for good reason. Two of its moves are fantastic together: Belly Drum and Drain Punch. Others like Thunder Punch and Close Combat can cover some more bases as well. I would choose an electric or fighting Tera Type for more power.

Koraidon

The other box legendary of this generation is also amazing and doesn't disappoint. It can boost itself with Swords Dance or weaken opponents with Screech, recover HP with Drain Punch, and win battles with the outstanding Collision Course move. Of course, a fighting Tera Type goes perfectly with this one.

Lucario

We all know how powerful (and cool) Lucario is, and this shift in generations didn't slow it down one bit. It's a solid physical sweeper with a great movepool that includes Extreme Speed, Close Combat, Meteor Mash and Swords Dance for an extra boost. I would not choose a defense-oriented Tera Type for this one - go all-out with fighting or steel.

Quaquaval

This is one great Pokémon if properly trained, since you first need to get one with the Moxie hidden ability and then complement its sweeper potential with Swords Dance. Aqua Step is the move you will want to abuse when possible. Other great options are Close Combat, Ice Spinner and U-Turn just in case of emergency. Water Tera Type is my first choice, but electric is also nice.

Tauros

I am very happy to see so many players out there using this amazing regional form. Since it can also get water or fire type with great moves like Rain Dance/Sunny Day and Flare Blitz/Surf, it is great for both single and double battles. Overcome its flying type weakness with a rock or steel Tera Type.

Bombirdier

This is a great generation for flying types, and this Pokémon is all the proof you need. It can disrupt with moves like Knock Off and Feather Dance, or do decent damage with moves like Rock Slide and Acrobatics. A rock Tera Type suits this one nicely.

Corviknight

The king of the skies in Galar might not be the best heavy hitter in Gen 9, but this Pokémon has found itself a good spot among supporters thanks to its amazing Mirror Armor ability and access to disruptive moves such as Screech, Fake Tears and Taunt. An electric Tera Type is a safe bet.

Flamigo

This is an amazing-looking Pokémon. Its type combination gives it a lot of weaknesses, but it can still give a few surprises thanks to its Scrappy ability and access to some great moves such as Brave Bird, Close Combat, U-Turn and Liquidation. Tera Type is flexible to counter weaknesses.

Gyarados

If you are a veteran of the series, you already know an Adamant Gyarados is something anyone will respect. You can choose an offensive strategy with Dragon Dance or just sweep with great moves such as Ice Fang, Aqua Tail and Crunch. It's kind of fragile, so try to choose a good Tera Type against rock or electric types.

Kilowattrel

This is a very speedy Pokémon capable of boosting easily thanks to its Competitive ability. It is straightforward to use too thanks to uncomplicated yet effective moves such as Thunderbolt, Air Slash, Volt Switch and Tera Blast. Water or steel Tera Types are great for this one.

Noivern

This is another great speedy Pokémon capable of taking the offensive right away with moves like Air Slash and Dragon Pulse. But it can also support others in double battles with moves like Tailwind. Its type combination makes it 4x weak against ice, so cover that with an appropriate Tera Type.

Oricorio

Another great option if you are looking for some type flexibility. Its Pom-Pom (electric) and Sensu (ghost) variations are popular, but you can train any of them for good results. Tera Type is flexible according to the variation you choose and the moves you teach it.

Salamence

Another great Pokémon capable of abusing the Moxie ability thanks to some amazing stats and the ability to boost even further with Dragon Dance. Dragon Rush and Aerial Ace are great moves for this one, but be sure to choose a Tera Type that will cover its 4x weakness to ice types.

Staraptor

This is a great physical sweeper and no doubt one of the most beloved flying types of the franchise. Choose high power moves such as Take Down, Brave Bird and Hurricane and take care of it switching when you're in a pinch. A rock Tera Type is great for this one.

Talonflame

This is another great sweeper option with the Flame Body agility at its disposal. It also has a few boosting options like Sunny Day and Swords Dance. Of course, Brave Bird is a must, and you can choose a steel Tera Type to solve its 4x weakness to rock types.

Banette

I love this Pokémon's design, and it is also really fun to use thanks to its various disrupting moves including Taunt and Will-O-Wisp. It is also a decent physical attacker with access to moves like Sucker Punch and Shadow Claw. A fairy Tera Type is a nice touch for this one.

Brambleghast

This Pokémon is kind of frail but a great option for double battles. I really like the Infestation/Grassy Terrain combo to support others. Unfortunately, this Pokémon has a lot of type disadvantages, so choose a Tera Type to counter what you're facing.

Drifblim

This Pokémon has great HP stat and decent attack, so you do have some opportunities to hit as it doesn't require a lot of setting up. Will-O-Wisp and Hex combo is a classic, but you can complement it with great moves like Air Slash and even Explosion for a nice surprise. I would use a ground Tera Type for this one.

Flutter Mane

This Pokémon has great special attack and defense, so it is another pretty easy to use ghost option for your team. Moonblast and Shadow Ball are your offensive options, and you can complement the strategy with moves like Fake Tears and Taunt. A dark or steel type Tera Type is great for this one.

Gengar

This is still a very fast and very strong special attacker that just lost gigantamaxing but is still a great option for any team. It has access to a diverse selection of moves that includes Focus Blast, Shadow Ball, Sludge Bomb and Dazzling Gleam, but you can also include some utility moves like Will-O-Wisp or Hypnosis. I like a dark or fairy Tera Type for a nice surprise.

Houndstone

Despite not having legendary stats, it holds its ground pretty well in both single and double battles thanks to powerful moves like Phantom Force and Shadow Ball. It also has access to Last Respects and the elemental fangs if you need more type coverage. Tera Type is flexible to cover for weaknesses.

Palossand

This Pokémon has a very interesting type combination making it a good defensive option for your team. Moves like Giga Drain, Confuse Ray and Stealth Rock make this one a very disruptive option as well. Tera Type is flexible to cover the weaknesses you're facing.

Polteageist

This is a great special sweeper option for your team, and I really like the advantage you can get from its Weak Armor ability. Shell Smash is a great choice too if you want to be even faster. Plus, you get access to great moves like Shadow Ball and Will-O-Wisp. I would go for a normal or fighting Tera Type.

Skeledirge

This is a fantastic ghost type for pretty much any situation. Torch Song is an amazing move that gets complemented with the Will-O-Wisp/Hex combo and Slack Off. It's a very powerful and balanced Pokémon and quite possibly my favorite of this generation. Fairy or water are the best Tera Type choices.

Spiritomb

This is a very defensive-oriented Pokémon that can be very annoying if you manage to keep it on the field long enough for its Pressure ability to make a difference. Dark Pulse and Foul Play are two of its best moves, and you can now easily compensate for its fairy type weakness with a poison or steel Tera Type.

Arboliva

How cool is this new Pokémon? It is also a decent special attacker with access to moves like Energy Ball, Hyper Voice and Earth Power. It works well in Sunny Day double battle teams if you're interested in that strategy. Be mindful of its many type weaknesses and choose the best Tera Type for your interests.

Brute Bonnet

I've been having a lot of fun with this one and it has already found its place among the best Pokémon of this generation. It hits hard, so go crazy with moves like Sucker Punch, Trash and even Giga Impact. Just be sure to choose a fire or flying Tera Type.

Gogoat

This Pokémon has the flexibility to make it a physical or special attacker according to your needs. It can also boost itself with moves like Growth and Grassy Terrain, which also makes this a great option for double battles. Try a rock Tera Type.

Jumpluff

This is another great option for Sunny Day teams as it has a couple abilities that take advantage of this weather condition nicely. It learns Poison Powder, Sleep Powder and Stun Spore, so you can also decide how you want to disrupt your opponent's strategy with this one. Steel or water Tera Types are great choices.

Leafeon

Yet another amazing choice for Sunny Day teams as it can choose between Leaf Guard or Chlorophyll abilities. It also has great stats, so teach it moves like Trailblaze, Leaf Blade and Tera Blast. Disrupt with Yawn or boost with Swords Dance. I've had great results with the ground Tera Type for further protection.

Lilligant

It's not the most efficient nor strong Pokémon by itself, but it can get very good fast if you take the time to boost it with moves such as Sunny Day and Quiver Dance. Energy Ball is great for this one, and it can also learn Synthesis for further durability. Tera Type is flexible.

Lurantis

It is a lot of fun using this one with its Contrary hidden ability. Plus, it is a decent physical attacker with great moves such as Leaf Blase, X-Scissor and Slash. Lurantis is pretty straightforward to use too, so just be careful that you choose the correct Tera Type for your needs.

Sawsbuck

Gotta love aesthetically pleasing Pokémon right? This one has a beautiful design no matter the season you choose to go with. Select physical moves like Double Kick, Double-Edge and Zen Headbutt to have a variety of types at your disposal. Tera Type is also flexible here.

Tsareena

An Adamant nature goes really well with this Pokémon since you want to boost its physical attack as much as possible. It also has access to some very nice moves like High Jump Kick, Acrobatics and Power Whip. You can go for a flying Tera Type for a nice extra surprise.

Wo-Chien

This is a scary Pokémon for its unique ability as well as the potential to trap and disrupt opponents with Mean Look and Knock Off. It Is also quite bulky, so it will not be easy taking this down unless there's some sort of powering-up involved. A ghost Tera Type works nicely with it.

Donphan

Sure, we have Paradox Pokémon now, but classic Donphan is still pretty strong! Its Sand Veil ability is great for Sandstorm teams, and you get some amazing hard-hitting moves as well, such as Bulldoze, Rapid Spin and Head Smash. A fire Tera Type is great to solve all of its type disadvantages.

Dugtrio

This is another great Pokémon for Sandstorm teams thanks to Sand Veil and an incredible Speed stat. It is also really simple to use with powerful and diverse moves such as Earthquake, Sucker Punch and Night Slash. Fire Tera Type will be a constant on this part of the list, but you can also opt to boost even further choosing ground.

Gastrodon

I have to admit this Pokémon is not as used as much as it was a few years ago, but the water/ground combination still hits hard. Muddy Water and Earth Power are great moves for this one, and you can also teach it Rain Dance for a bit more utility. Go for a fire or grass Tera Type.

Hippowdon

If you're going for a Sandstorm team, then you know Hippowdon is a great choice as the first Pokémon thanks to its Sand Stream ability. Of course, it can hit hard with moves like Earthquake, Rock Slide and Ice Fang, but I also like to teach Yawn to it to disrupt a bit and force switches. Both fire or ice Tera Types work great.

Krookodile

I really like using its Anger Point hidden ability as this can become really dangerous quickly. It can boost with Hone Claws or disrupt with Torment, but you usually want to hit with powerful moves such as Earthquake or Crunch. Its type combination has a few disadvantages, so choose a Tera Type accordingly.

Mudsdale

This is a great physical attacker with access to a variety of moves that can cover some bases when battling. My favorite moves for this one are High Horsepower, Rock Smash and Heavy Slam. You can make it a bit sturdier too with Iron Defense. Tera Type is flexible.

Sandaconda

This is a very defense-oriented Pokémon capable of disruptions and a great support for Sandstorm teams as well. Moves like Coil and Glare are great to complement other heavy hitting ones like Brutal Swing and Drill Run. Choose a Tera Type that will boost resistance against its natural water and grass weaknesses.

Ting-Lu

This has got to be one of the best defensive Pokémon of this generation thanks to its unique ability. It can also deal some damage with devastating moves like Throat Chop, Rock Slide and Earthquake. Go for an offensive Tera Type to boost these moves even further.

Toedscruel

I just love this new Pokémon's concept, and despite not having the best stats, it is still pretty fun to use! I like battling with mine using Hex, Spore, Earth Power and Leaf Storm to have a good utility balance, but you can also try some other moves like Grassy Terrain or Energy Ball. Go for a fire Tera Type for this one.

Whiscash

Still a very interesting and very fun Pokémon to use, and it also hits quite hard with moves like Aqua Tail, Giga Impact and Earthquake. Of course, you can also use Rain Dance or incorporate it to your current Rain Dance team. A fire Tera Type is suggested here.

Abomasnow

This is a great Pokémon that summons a hailstorm when it enters battle, so of course it is a great choice if you're using some kind of Ice-type strategy. Has access to powerful moves such as Ice Punch and Wood Hammer, with some utility ones such as Swagger and Ingrain. Go for a water Tera Type to avoid 1-hit KOs.

Avalugg

Pure ice-types tend to be kind of frail, but Avalugg has the tools to ensure its survivability with the Ice Body ability, great defense, and the Iron Defense move. Once you feel comfortable, you can start attacking with moves like Icicle Crash, Heavy Slam and Crunch. A Dragon Tera Type makes it a bit sturdier.

Beartic

Another great Pokémon for hailstorm teams thanks to its Slush Rush ability. It is best suited as a physical attacker, so go for moves like Icicle Crash, Giga Impact and Close Combat. You could also try to increase its survivability with Rest and/or Swagger. Tera Type is flexible for this one.

Cetitan

Try to train one with the Sheer Force hidden ability. This Pokémon does not have the best defenses, so you want to make sure it deals some big damage before it goes down. You have great moves at your disposal such as Body Slam, Avalanche and Bounce. You can try to boost its defenses with Amnesia as well. A fire Tera Type works well.

Chien-Pao

The Sword of Ruin ability is great for this very fast, very powerful Pokémon. As a Legendary, you know it has great stats, so boost your attack with Swords Dance as much as possible before dealing enormous damage with moves like Ruination and Ice Spinner. A flying Tera Type is recommended here.

Cryogonal

This Pokémon has great Special Defense, so it might be what you need for your hailstorm team. Aurora Veil and Haze are amazing defensive moves to have on this one, and you can also do a bit of damage with other moves like Ancient Power and Freeze-Dry. A water or rock Tera Type is great here.

Frosmoth

The Ice Scales hidden ability can provide this Pokémon with a bit more protection, which it needs so it can get the job done. It is also best suited as a special attacker with moves like Blizzard, Bug Buzz and Hurricane. Just be mindful of its 4x weakness against Fire and Rock types. Choose a water Tera Type to solve this issue.

Glaceon

This very cute, very strong eeveelution focuses on Special Attack, and so Calm Mind is its most useful tool. Try to protect this Pokémon as much as possible while it boosts itself, and then sweep with Icy Wind or Tera Blast. A fire Tera Type is recommended to give your opponent a nice surprise.

Glalie

This is a really balanced Pokémon that is also easy to use with a great variety of moves that include Crunch, Frost Breath and Weather Ball. You can also disrupt a bit with Disable and Protect. A fire Tera Type is also nice here too.

Iron Bundle

This is one terrifying Santa to face thanks to its amazing stats and a very powerful selection of moves to deal with any situation, like Hydro Pump, Freeze-Dry and Ice Beam, plus some disruption thanks to Disable and Encore. Choose between ice or water Tera type for great damage output.

Blissey

This Pokémon is a tank with a great special defense and the capacity to boost its survivability even further with Light Screen and Soft-Boiled. It is also capable of some disruptions thanks to moves like Sing. Its only real weakness is the fighting type, which is very popular these days, so I recommend a psychic or flying Tera Type.

Braviary

An Adamant-natured specimen with the Defiant hidden ability is the way to go to maximize damage. Cover various types with moves like Brave Bird, Crush Claw and Superpower to build a pretty straightforward and fun Pokémon to use. A rock Tera Type works really well with this one.

Dudunsparce

Of course, I had to include the evolution of my favorite in the list. It is still not the majestic creature we have envisioned for years, but it still gets some love with a useful variety of moves like Drill Run, Tera Blast and Dragon Tail. It is really a jack of all trades and hilarious to use and win with. I suggest a flying Tera Type.

Farigiraf

Talk about a deserved evolution! This is a decent special attacker that can boost itself nicely with the aid of Calm Mind and Nasty Plot, and it can get some time to achieve this with utility moves like Thunder Wave. I suggest a flying Tera type for this one as well.

Greedent

This Pokémon has great HP and special defense stats, and both of its abilities are great when equipping a berry to it. Of course, you can keep the food-themed fun going with Stockpile, Spit Up and Swallow. Bet your foes won't be expecting that huh? A psychic Tera Type works well to counter fighting types.

Maushold

Believe me when I say you'll have a ton of fun training and battling with this one. Its Technician hidden ability boosts the Beat Up move more than you would imagine, and you can complement with some others like Play Rough and Bullet Seed. Use a normal Tera Type for some extra laughs.

Oinkologne

Be sure to choose a favorable nature to make it work well (Adamant is ideal). I really like to start off with Yawn and then boost a bit with Work-Up. Then you have access to decent moves from various types including Play Rough, Chilling Water and Zen Headbutt. Go for a psychic Tera Type for this one.

Pyroar

This Pokémon is great because of its Moxie hidden ability and the Noble Roar move combo. Both work together to make this a great special attacker with access to moves like Dark Pulse, Overheat and Hyper Voice. I would really go for the offensive route and choose a fire Tera Type as well.

Slaking

I do not see how Truant is a disadvantage for this Pokémon being the beast that it is. Some people prefer to use Vigoroth, but when you hit with moves like Play Rough, Giga Impact and Drain Punch, you learn the true potential of this Pokémon. It is so powerful that I recommend giving it a normal Tera Type to boost even further.

Ursaring

Word on the street is we are getting access to Ursaluna when Scarlet/Violet become compatible with Pokémon Bank. Meanwhile, you can have a ton of fun with this one as a powerful physical sweeper by teaching it moves like Hammer Arm, Play Rough and Slash. You can go for a more defensive route too with Rest, but I still recommend a normal Tera Type.

Amoonguss

We all know this is one of the most useful Pokémon out there. It has been a vital part of many champions' teams and for good reason. It is full of surprises and a great support for double battles that can learn Spore, Clear Smog and Grassy Terrain. Tera Type is very flexible also so that's another plus for this Pokémon.

Clodsire

I loved this Pokémon from the first time I trained it since it is very useful in both single and double battles. Toxic, Stealth Rock and Recover are going to be your main tools. The last one is an offensive option such as Earthquake. Mine has poison Tera Type and it works great.

Dragalge

This is another great choice for rookie players since you can just go for a simple build and try out moves like Dragon Pulse, Sludge Bomb and Water Pulse. Of course, the addition of Toxic can also help. Use a poison Tera Type here as well.

Grafaiai

I like building this one as a mischievous, disruptive Pokémon with moves like Knock Off, Flatter and Toxic. Be sure to also give it the Prankster hidden ability to make it more effective. Tera Type is flexible, but focus on defending against super effective types.

Iron Moth

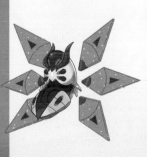

I really was not expecting this to be a poison type, but I am glad it is! It has great stats, so you do not really need to worry about boosting too much. Just go for variety with Sludge Wave, Flamethrower, Energy Ball and Dazzling Gleam, and just like that you now have a very flexible special sweeper! I like the grass Tera Type here.

Muk

One of these with the Poison Touch ability can really deal some damage in the long run. It is pretty sturdy with access to Acid Armor, Disable and Minimize, so this is a great choice if you want to play the long game. A steel Tera Type is suggested here.

Salazzle

This is quite the fast special attacker with typical moves like Fire Blast and Venoshock, but you can also make this a more utility-oriented Pokémon with moves like Swagger, Toxic and Torment. It is 4x weak to ground types, so go for a water or grass Tera Type.

Swalot

This can be another great defensive-oriented Pokémon for your team. It has great stats, and it is pretty sturdy. Plus, Swalot has access to moves like Yawn, Encore and Stockpile, so you can play the long game safely with this one as part of your team. A dark Tera Type is recommended.

Toxicroak

This has always been a really fun and aggressive choice if you like punching Pokémon. I like mine with Toxic, Poison Jab and Brick Break. You can also disrupt a bit with options like Taunt. Of course, it is 4x weak against psychic, so you need the dark Tera Type to be on the safe side.

Toxtricity

How cool is this type combo? Its Punk Rock ability goes well with moves like Boomburst, but you can ignore this and go for more classic choices such as Electric Terrain and Discharge. Be wary of ground types, so protect your Pokémon with a water or grass Tera Type.

Espathra
This Pokémon is quite interesting since it has a great exclusive move called Lumina Crash that goes really well with Calm Mind and Psychic Terrain. It is a pretty fast Pokémon, so even if it's facing something dangerous you should be able to hit first. Tera Type is flexible for this one.

Hypno
This is a pretty straightforward Pokémon to use. It has great Special Defense, so you can boost a couple turns with Calm Mind or Nasty Plot, and then use moves like Psychic, Focus Blast and Tera Blast. You can also disrupt a bit with Swagger or Hypnosis. A fairy Tera Type is nice here.

Espeon
You've got to love powerful yet easy to use Pokémon such as Espeon. It has access to Calm Mind and Stored Power, which makes it really devastating. Add Dazzling Gleam for some dark-type protection and you're good to go. You can leave a psychic Tera Type on this one as well.

Medicham
This is a speedy option with a great type combination that can cover many bases in your team. I like mine with Work Up, Fake Out, Brick Break and Zen Headbutt, but it can also learn the elemental punches if you need variety. Tera Type is flexible.

Golduck
You could choose one of these with the Cloud Nine ability to disrupt weather teams, or you can also boost your own weather team with moves like Rain Dance and Confuse Ray. This one works better in doubles, so that is where I would recommend it. A fire Tera Type is a fun surprise for your opponents.

Oranguru
One of these with the Telepathy ability is great for double battles. It can use Calm Mind and Stored Power but also has access to great utility moves like Yawn, Taunt and Light Screen. I like a fire Tera Type to protect it against its bug weakness.

Gothitelle
This one has great Special Defense and also has access to the Shadow Tag ability, which is fun. Light Screen and Calm Mind can improve its survivability, and a move like Stored Power is a must with these conditions. Tera Type is flexible according to what you are facing.

Slowking
It is not getting as much love as Slowbro these days, but I still think it is a great, bulky option with some big damage capabilities. It can use Trick Room and Rain Dance to boost itself or a teammate, and it's sturdy enough to switch it out so it can set up strategy again later in the game. Tera Type is flexible to cover for weaknesses.

Grumpig
This is another great defense-oriented Pokémon that can learn Light Screen and Confuse Ray for some on-field fun. Bounce, Stored Power and Dazzling Gleam are great move choices to take advantage of your setups. Choose a fighting or flying Tera Type here.

Veluza
A great Pokémon with an exclusive move, Fillet Away, that boosts 3 different stats with HP cost. You can expect it to hit hard and fast so just complement with moves like Aqua Cutter, Psycho Cut and Night Slash and see those big damage numbers. Tera Type can be an offensive one according to your preference.

Coalossal

This was one of my favorite Pokémon from Gen 8 and I am glad we still have access to it these days. It is very sturdy and fantastically strong. It can set up Sandstorm, but you mainly want to teach it strong moves like Heat Crash and Stone Edge. It is 4x weak against water and ground types, so go for a grass type for a nice surprise.

Drednaw

Great for Rain Dance teams if you can get its Swift Swim ability. It can boost itself with Rock Polish and attack with Stone Edge and Razor Shell. Scary Face is great to level the field in terms of speed. It is 4x weak to grass, so go for a flying Tera Type.

Garganacl

This is a highly defensive Pokémon capable of doing some important damage thanks to its exclusive move Salt Cure. You can instead go for a utility moveset including Stealth Rock, Recover, Stone Edge and Earthquake. It is simple, yet really effective. A dragon Tera Type counters pretty much all of its type disadvantages.

Glimmora

It is a great utility Pokémon thanks to its Toxic Debris ability, it can also learn Stealth Rock and then continue causing some more damage with moves like Energy Ball, Earth Power and Power Gem to cover a wide variety of type necessities. A flying Tera Type is recommended here.

Iron Thorns

This is another great physical attacker with access to a variety of move types that can do some big damage. I like mine with Stone Edge, Wild Charge, Ice Punch and Earthquake, but there are many more options according to what you are facing. An offensive Tera Type for your favorite move is also suggested.

Klawf

A defense-oriented Pokémon with means to becoming even a stronger tank with access to Iron Defense. And also capable of some utility thanks to Knock-Off and Sandstorm. For damage, I suggest Stone Edge and Rock Smash. Tera Type is flexible according to what you're facing.

Lycanroc

Another great choice for your Sandstorm team with different stats depending on the form you are choosing. No matter your favorite, you can be sure it is a great offensive Pokémon with moves like Rock Slide, Crunch and Counter. Tera Type is flexible here too.

Stonjourner

A great and sturdy choice for double battles with access to the very useful move Gravity, as well as some other solid choices like Stone Edge and Heavy Slam. It can learn Curse if you need to boost even further. It has quite a few weaknesses so choose a Tera Type to cover for this.

Sudowoodo

Be mindful that this Pokémon is quite slow, but packs a powerful punch. The Rattled ability helps, but it is quite situational, so I would not depend on it. On the bright side, it can cover many bases with moves like Wood Hammer, Rock Tomb and Flail (a must have if you go for the Sturdy ability). Tera Type is flexible.

Tyranitar

The Sand Stream ability is what makes this Pokémon a must have in Sandstorm teams. It is also a quite powerful physical attacker with extra durability. Taunt, Crunch and Stone Edge are three great move choices with a flex one for your needs. It is 4x weak to fighting, so a psychic or flying Tera Type is your best bet.

Bronzong

Durability is the name of the game when you play with this. It has great defensive stats and moves to boost them like Calm Mind and Reflect. Plus, Bronzong is also a great disruptor with solid choices like Rain Dance, Metal Sound and Extrasensory. Going for a dark Tera Type is also a nice surprise for your opponent.

Copperajah

Quite a straightforward choice if you like simplicity and great damage. This one can really shine with powerful moves like Heavy Slam, High Horsepower and Play Rough, covering quite a lot of your type needs. A ground Tera Type is suggested here.

Gholdengo

This is quite a hard Pokémon to evolve but so worth it! It has amazing stats and can really play its own game with a good move combination, including Thunder Wave, Trick, Shadow Ball and Make It Rain. There's no point in going defensive here, so go ahead and stick with a steel Tera Type.

Iron Treads

Yet another great choice for offense. This Paradox Pokemon is quite strong and doesn't really need to boost, but can have some utility with moves like Rapid Spin and Knock Off. Then, sweep with Earthquake and Iron Head. Choose a ground Tera Type here for some extra power that can give you some one-hit Knock-Outs.

Kingambit

One of the most popular Pokémon from this generation, and also has some great stats and moves to back up this statement. Its signature move Kowtow Cleave is amazing, and you can complement with Iron Head, Sucker Punch and Brick Break. A flying Tera Type works nicely.

Klefki

I have to admit this one lost a bit of popularity thanks to Tinkaton, but it is still a solid choice if you happen to train one of these instead. It has great utility with moves like Torment and Magic Room, and it can stand its own ground with Flash Cannon and Dazzling Gleam. A water Tera Type covers its main weaknesses.

Magnezone

Quite simple to use and yet really effective in pretty much any kind of battle. Thunderbolt, Flash Cannon and Volt Switch are the three main moves for this one. I would recommend Tera Blast for the very last one. Choose a grass Tera Type and you are covering many bases with ease.

Orthworm

This can be a very tricky Pokémon to face, so you might want to train one for the fun of it. I like it as a Stealth Rock and Spikes user, with other fun choices like Shed Tail and Body Press. A fairy Tera Type works great with this one.

Revavroom

No need to overcomplicate things with this Pokemon. It hits hard and can be a great attacker with good type coverage with moves like Iron Head, Gunk Shot, Bulldoze and Shift Gear to give it an extra bit of power. It is 4x weak against ground types, so a grass Tera Types goes nicely here.

Scizor

A lack of Mega Evolution didn't stop this one from being a valuable and amazing physical attacker for the current gen. You probably already know some of its best moves like U-Turn and Bullet Punch, but you can also complement with options like Thief and Quick Attack. Stick with the steel Tera Type here.

Barraskewda

This is quite the speedy Pokémon, and I like incorporating it into my Rain Dance team since it can learn the move itself, but that is not a must. Crunch, Aqua Jet and Throat Chop are some of its best moves. A grass Tera Type goes nicely with it.

Clawitzer

This is a fine choice if you are looking for a special attacker with access to moves from several types. It can learn Water Pulse, Dragon Pulse and Aqua Sphere, so you have quite decent coverage here. You can also teach it Tera Blast and go for a grass Tera Type to complement nicely.

Cloyster

This Pokémon is still one impressive option after all these years, and I love using it anytime. Train one with the Skill Link ability and start things off with Shell Smash, then sweep away with Icicle Spear, Rock Blast and Drill Run. Easy and fun! It is quite weak, but I would still suggest you go for ice or rock Tera Type.

Dodonzo

This has great resistance to physical moves and can become a true wall if you let it play out. Curse is its main source of survivability, and I like using Body Press, Earthquake and Wave Crash to complete the moveset. A ground or fighting Tera Type is suggested.

Floatzel

It has great speed and decent Attack and Special Attack stats, so it is quite flexible for all kinds of battles. It learns Rain Dance, so that is always an option. Other great move choices are Aqua Jet, Ice Fang and Tera Blast. A fire Tera Type works well with this one.

Lumineon

This is a decent Pokémon for double battles since it can enable others with moves like Tailwind and Safeguard. You can also include more offensive choices like Surf, Bounce and U-Turn to cover many common types. Tera Type is flexible.

Palafin

The Hero Form of Palafin is an amazing Pokémon but, of course, you need to work a bit for it. I recommend using Flip Turn right away and have it change form to be available to battle at its full potential. Wave Crash, Ice Punch and Close Combat are available for the great hero's return. Keep the water Tera Type for extra power.

Slowbro

It is quite popular for Raid Battles these days, but it's also an excellent choice to face other trainers. It can boost itself with Iron Defense and Nasty Plot, and attack with Stored Power and Water Pulse. Tera Type for this one is flexible.

Toxapex

This Pokémon has great defense and the means to survive for quite a long time if you let it work. Baneful Bunker and Toxic are great moves, and can be complemented well with Chilling Water and Poison Jab. It can also learn Haze, which is really useful. A flying Tera Type is also nice for this one.

Vaporeon

One of the best defensive eeveelutions in the game is supported by great stats and very useful moves like Wish, Yawn and Protect. Since it is very good defending itself, I would keep the water Tera Type for extra power on an offensive move of your choosing.

Pokémon Colosseum and Pokémon XD: Gale of Darkness

Were these games ahead of their time?

By Angel Pelaez

I am aware the vast majority of you are too young to have played the Pokémon games on systems like the Nintendo 64 or the GameCube. So let me tell you this: there were some amazing ideas in those systems that were buried under the sands of time. This might have been for the best though, since those times were like the awkward teenage years of the Pokémon franchise. However, the recent launch of Pokémon Scarlet & Violet really left me thinking about a couple of these games, specifically Pokémon Colosseum, launched in 2003 and Pokémon XD: Gale of Darkness, launched in 2005. I really think these were games ahead of their time.

Let's see if we can awaken your curiosity for games that are probably older than you, shall we? This should be interesting to say the least.

Pokémon Colosseum had a very particular premise: the ability to catch another trainer's Pokémon. Who has not tried this before? Have you considered what the consequences would be? That would be considered a Pokémon crime, don't you think? The Orre region was a dystopia of shady themes and characters. This region was quite different from what we had seen in Pokemon before. Imagine a Mad Max concept for Pokémon and you would not be that far from what this region looks like: a desertic, harsh world where Pokémon are tools, not partners.

You start the game as a bad guy. You are a member of Team Snagem (a quite darker version of Team Rocket that is actually successful), and your job is to steal other trainers' Pokémon for the organization. You are also very successful at it, but one day you have a change of heart and decide to steal one of the snag machines (a contraption that allows Poké Balls to capture other trainers' Pokémon) to seek justice for those poor Pokémon and the trainers that lost them.

The story reminds me of other wild west based stories. It's a very mature concept full of moral dilemmas that evolve as you play the campaign. And it gets better...

This game had clear influences from games like Final Fantasy VII. Genius Sonority, the developers behind this game, presented a mature story aimed for an audience that had aged through 3 different generations of Pokémon. For them, the time was right to set a darker tone.

Pokémon Colosseum was launched on Nintendo's home console, which meant it was one of the very few Pokémon games that couldn't be played on the go (but the GameCube was a fairly portable console at the time, to be fair).

Let's circle back to the Orre region once more, which I just described as a wild west setting for a pretty cool Pokémon Adventure, right? Back then, it was everything but that. We were used to lush and varied locations Pokémon could call home. But the once technological and glorious Orre region was barren, with

no wild Pokémon on sight, only half-destroyed towns with a handful of people separated by quite a cruel desert. Your means of transport was a pretty cool bike, similar to what you'd find in a Star Wars movie in a desert setting.

The opening segments pair you with a couple Pokémon: Espeon and Umbreon, already evolved and leveled up with moves already selected for you. It was not the clean canvas we were used to getting, nor were you at the liberty to choose a Pokémon partner. It was a matter of working with what you had at the moment.

The story of course wouldn't have been fully realized without the presence of strong and well-written characters. Some of these were nightmare material (I recommend doing a quick search for Miror B. and his Pokéball afro!). The designers of this game really went all out and tried many different inspirations, designs, sizes and personalities. They had limited resources back then, and still came up with some amazing characters and Pokémon designs that were truly impressive. Everything was of course accompanied by an amazing soundtrack that included songs to fit all moods.

But what did Team Snagem do with the stolen Pokémon? If you've played Pokémon Go, you know about Shadow Pokémon, and this was where that concept came from. The Pokémon would go to another organization, the much more villainous Team Cipher, who would corrupt these Pokémon in order to increase their raw power by closing their hearts to any emotion, rendering them incapable of feeling and turning them into the perfect battle tools that would obey any command without remorse.

Pokémon Colosseum and Pokémon XD: Gale of Darkness

PERR: I won't tell your parents, so don't rat me out to my grandpa, okay?

was quite probably the most difficult Pokémon game to beat. You had to use Pokémon with preset moves. These Pokemon were already evolved or under-leveled. It was a matter of adapting to what you had while battling against a quite strong AI. A single Pokémon battle could go for as long as 50 minutes, an insane idea even for today's standards. As you progressed, you would be facing Pokémon like Raikou, Entei, and Suicune. All of these were outstanding Pokémon.

There was also a very difficult version of "Mount Battle" with 100 trainer battles to overcome on top of a volcano. Conquering this was the ultimate flex back then! Winning rewarded you with a very cool Shadow Ho-Oh.

Genius Sonority absolutely nailed the darker tone with this game. They took what was beloved from the first three generations of portable games, mixing them with the 3D graphics and animations from the Pokémon Stadium games and the influence from other media to deliver one of the most fresh and unique Pokémon games to date.

This game had a successor just 2 years after called Pokémon XD: Gale of Darkness. The story takes place 5 years after Colosseum with a new, friendlier protagonist tasked with the same mission to rescue and purify Shadow Pokémon and end Team Cipher's malicious schemes. You went out to a more traditional Pokémon adventure, taking on grunts and admins as you dismantled Team Cipher little by little.

This was a much more polished game with clear influence of the fans' feedback from the first game. The user interface was cleaner, and you could even capture 9 different wild Pokémon in specific places called Poké Spots, all of which could be traded for rare Pokémon. There were also 83 Shadow Pokémon to catch this time around, and a new alternative method to purify Shadow Pokémon.

This game gave us the very cool and intimidating Shadow Lugia and one of the scariest Pokémon trainers I have ever faced: Master Greevil. And despite this being a cheesier story compared to its predecessor, it was a well-driven story with potential for yet another sequel that never came to exist.

The reception of Pokémon XD: Gale of Darkness was not as great as its predecessor's, as many of the ideas and assets were recycled from the previous game and

The fact that this is so similar to Pokémon Go's own Shadow Pokémon is proof of the fantastic yet ahead of its time idea. It talks to the player about abuse and the power of greed over compassion. These Pokémon were as fierce back then as they are right now. You had a great desire to save and purify them so they could get a second chance. It was about that glimmer of hope in the middle of all this chaos and hopelessness.

So, this is where you started using your snag machine. You were only able to steal Shadow Pokémon from other trainers among the ranks of Team Snagem and Team Cipher. There were only 48 Shadow Pokémon to encounter and steal back, which was quite a limited number compared to the 386 Pokémon available at the time.

Of course, the main objective for stealing these Pokémon was to reopen their hearts so they could be purified again. It was about rescuing them more than stealing them.

There is one reason why Pokémon Colosseum is popular among long-time veterans: the difficulty. This

did not feature a mature story like we were expecting. It also did not take many risks and just constructed on what worked last time around, which is probably why we never saw another game similar to these two.

Many years have passed, and I am wondering here: What if Nintendo suddenly announced a remake for any of these games, or both? Would they be accepted and valued by a new generation of gamers? And I believe the answer would be a definitive YES. They already remade Pokémon Snap. But Colosseum and Gale of Darkness represented the vision of a different studio that transformed the traditionally friendly Pokémon concept into a more mature story that would fit perfectly with the much more mature audience we are today. It would be a great opportunity to experiment with the series having a more serious tone.

Maybe we will get to play these GameCube games again sometime in the future, but I don't really see these as a priority for the potential catalog. Despite not having hopes for these games, I still want to reflect on what they did for the franchise and how these games were truly ahead of their time, paving way for some really cool ideas we got later on.

I already mentioned Shadow Pokémon being on Pokémon Go, but the other cool feature that these games provided to the main series is the ability to trade and/or transfer Pokémon to the main games of the series. Having your purified Pokémon stuck in a GameCube memory card was kind of sad, but having them help you out with your battles on the GameBoy Advance games? Now that was so cool. I believe this idea evolved into software like Pokémon Transfer, Pokémon Band and Pokémon Home. It is still possible to have your GameCube Pokémon transferred all the way to Pokémon Home.

Of course, these were the first games to also have a fully realized 3D adventure way before we could get this possibility on the Nintendo 3DS. It was a barren world, pretty much empty, but it ran great given the limitations of the time.

These Pokémon games really provided a challenge that no other game in the main RPG series has offered since. We really miss the Battle Frontier these days, when we were really challenged by superb AI, and I am hopeful we might get a more challenging Artificial Intelligence again sometime in the future.

There was also the cool concept of getting Pokémon from outside sources. Some copies of these games came with bonus discs that granted Pokémon like Jirachi. We also had a neat gadget to read physical cards on the GameBoy Advance called the E-Card Reader, from which we could get Togepi and Scizor. (This is not so different from promo codes you can get at your favorite retailer to download a Pokemon even these days.)

It might be difficult for you to get a chance to play these games since copies are fairly hard to come by. But I suggest you look for some playthroughs and guides online to get a grip of what these games were about. They were amazing games and contributed to what makes Pokémon great today. They do not get the recognition they deserve.

Pokémon Scarlet & Violet Review

By Angel Pelaez

A few months have passed since the launch of Pokémon Scarlet & Violet, and we know the launch was a little rough for Generation 9. There were a bunch of technical problems and bugs that prevented many players from enjoying the new Pokémon generation properly.

Some players focused on the bad stuff at the time, instead of looking beyond launch. So, I am doing something odd here, reviewing a game that launched in November 2022. Because it truly deserves a chance to be seen for more than it was at launch.

So, let us dig in and see if we can see things from a different angle, shall we?

Go wherever you want to go — This was the premise given for these new games at launch. At last, Pokémon games with a true open world with no limitations for where you could go or a set order of tasks to complete the game. It was truly a dream for long-time Pokémon fans. Despite still having some limitations that kept us from exploring the whole map or challenging the league right away, it mostly delivered on this front.

And it was truly amazing. I had unbelievable luck finding a shiny Lechonk just 10 minutes after starting my adventure, so this new sense of discovery really struck me hard from the very beginning of the game. Suddenly, I wanted to explore more, I wanted to see more of the map and got lost constantly, forgetting about the main route and just wandering off to see

new Pokémon or strong trainers that were way off the beaten path.

The map itself offers a good variety of biomes and it is bigger than what we saw in Galar. You will encounter many Pokémon with different and believable behaviors; for example, Tauros will attack you on sight while Psyduck will just stare at your soul without moving a muscle. We got a glimpse of this "living world" back in Pokémon Legends Arceus, but it was definitely more polished this time around.

Circling back to the main objective of the game, there are actually three of them. As a brand-new student of the Uva or Naranja Academy (depending on your version of the game), you will be tasked with a hunt to find your own treasure and have an adventure that is truly your own. You are quickly introduced to three paths: one to become a Pokémon League Champion, one to help a friend gather mysterious cooking ingredients from massive Titan Pokémon, and one more to help disband a team of rogue academy students.

Between these three main paths, there are a total of 18 activities. You will be taking on all 18 types of Pokémon which is pretty cool since they all get a bit of love and time in the spotlight, and some of the later-game activities really show off the potential of some very strong trainers and Pokémon.

I have to say I really enjoyed the classic route of 8 gyms spread across the map, with very charismatic and interesting gym leaders and some extraordinary Pokémon battles. Each gym now has a previous test that goes from Pokémon hide-and-seek to participating in a streaming show. All of these definitely add up to the fantastic script throughout the story.

Your main partner here is actually your rival: Nemona, who is actually a Pokémon League Champion already (there can be more than one this time around). Nemona is always excited about your gym progress. She pops up every once in a while to give you useful information about the league, and also challenges you to see how much you have improved. I have to say the very last match between champions was an amazing one that I really enjoyed quite a lot. She is adorable and

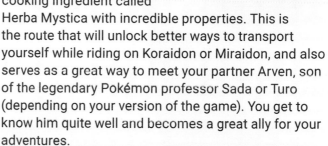

energetic. There is never a bad vibe between the player and Nemona. She just wants you to be great so she can face off against someone with all her might.

The second route sends you looking for Titan Pokémon in order to retrieve a legendary cooking ingredient called Herba Mystica with incredible properties. This is the route that will unlock better ways to transport yourself while riding on Koraidon or Miraidon, and also serves as a great way to meet your partner Arven, son of the legendary Pokémon professor Sada or Turo (depending on your version of the game). You get to know him quite well and becomes a great ally for your adventures.

The last route has you battling against Team Star, the "baddies" of these games. They are dispersed all across Paldea and have settled into bases for you to conquer. The team leaders are colorful and amazingly well scripted. They are also some of the toughest battles I had.

These bases also make use of a new mechanic called the Go Feature, which lets you take out the first three Pokémon in your party from their Pokéballs and battle against Team Star's in quick battles before a set timer runs out. Note that this Go Feature can also be used anywhere in Paldea, and battling wild Pokémon gives a small amount of Exp and some Pokémon materials to build TMs. I wouldn't call this the most entertaining route, but it was certainly the hardest one, so it's perfect for those looking for a challenge. Penny is the character that will be tagging along with you during this mission, and she has a very nice secret that's unveiled at the end of this route.

Once you complete the main three routes, a fourth one involving the Central Crater of Paldea opens. Here, the mysterious Area Zero will serve as a new place for discovery as the only place where you can encounter Paradox Pokémon. You also get to reach a conclusion about this place, the relationship between Arven and his mother or father, and the Terastal

The whole story is fantastic in my opinion. And I really wish they had incorporated voice acting into it, it's THAT good.

When it is all said and done, the true end game begins. You complete your Pokédex of course, and then you start to learn the ropes at competitive Pokémon breeding and training, Picnics and their influence on Pokémon outbreaks, and shiny hunting, requiring a good investment of time and resources to test out your favorites in online competitions. But you can also take the PvE (player vs. environment) route in the form of Tera Raids, a direct evolution of the Max Raid Battles we found in Gen 8, but quite a bit harder.

Taking on 1-4 star raids is simple enough to do alone, but 5 and 6 star raids are where your Pokémon will really be tested. You really need fully trained, level 100 Pokémon to tackle these by yourself (or in co-op) to have a chance to capture Pokémon with great stats and a rare Tera Type. There are even limited time 7-star Tera Raids that demand strategy and some level of coordination between players. So far, Cinderace and Charizard have been introduced to the game via these raids, and more are sure to come.

I have to make a quick special recognition of the game's fantastic soundtrack. Each track is so energetic and full of personality that it truly elevates the experience of every town, gym battle, or legendary encounter. Be sure to enjoy every track because they are all amazing.

Of course, we have to talk about the technical issues flooding the games at launch. Pokémon Scarlet & Violet are the least polished games in the series by far. They are pretty rough experiences due to a lot of bugs present in the base games.

We are talking about inconsistent frame rates, models popping in and out of the screen at very short distances, and processing times that can really become a nuisance when doing something so simple as checking out your Pokédex or the Pokémon in your boxes.

Phenomenon. All your buddies will be here by your side, participating in the most dramatic part of the game and serving as true partners up to the moment where the credits roll.

But wait, there's more! You are then asked to rematch each of the Gym Leaders with much stronger and competitive Pokémon at their disposal, finishing off with a tournament that involves all of the Academy's teachers and students. By this point your Pokémon will be around level 85, and you certainly feel a sense of accomplishment, of true growth with your Pokémon.

You can also go to school to meet a colorful cast of teachers, take some classes that give out some decent knowledge and rewards, and form bonds with the people living and teaching on campus. This also creates a mini side quest to look for the other legendaries of these games.

The new Union Circle, a way to fully enter another player's game and play co-op for up to 4 players, is a fantastic idea that, unfortunately, is the least playable part of these games. It is slow and painful to play with your friends, and I am really hoping this gets patched up soon.

Nintendo has acknowledged these problems and promised to fix the games as soon as possible. A couple patches have been released since then, but Scarlet and Violet are still very rough experiences at the time I write this.

But there is a bright side of this, and it's a comforting fact for those who, like me, stick with these games for years and play the game competitively: Pokemon battles work perfectly. Player and Pokémon models look great, animations are fantastic and the core experience is a solid one. If the new terastallizing mechanics were broken or the Pokémon battles themselves were unplayable, we would definitely have reasons to panic. There is hope for the future and these games should be fixed, at least partially. Even if they cannot patch everything, these games serve as a very solid foundation for a 10th generation sometime in the future.

Never before have we had Pokémon games be this ambitious. We have the same base of an amazing RPG game, a great story with very likable characters, and a superb soundtrack to go with it. But the developers have incorporated new strategies, moves, Pokémon and mechanics to the equation. It's big and complex, but it's balanced.

Scarlet and Violet are great games for long-time fans. They are also very fun games for younger fans and casual audiences. These are the open world Pokémon games we have been dreaming about since the first time we saw Pokémon in 3D back in Pokémon Stadium. They are not perfect, nor they will be called a masterpiece anytime soon, but I think we will get to see their value as the stepping stone for future generations of Pokémon.

This is reason enough for me to recommend these games, and they are fully enjoyable whether you decide to only complete the main games or if, like me, you will end up spending hundreds of hours building teams for online competition. We truly have a couple of solid games for everyone to enjoy. So, hop in if you have not already! There is still a lot to discover and more Pokémon to catch on the horizon.

Ranking the Pokémon games

What are the best and worst generations?

By Angel Pelaez

It is incredible to think that we have lived through nine generations of Pokémon games. What started with a simple choice between Bulbasaur, Charmander and Squirtle quickly evolved to become a true global phenomenon. Pokémon is present in all sorts of media and merchandise all over the world, and faces like Pikachu are recognized by pretty much everyone around the world.

This would not have been possible without the main Pokémon games. All of them have added new species, new mechanics and new exciting sights to explore and conquer. It seems like the quest to become a true Pokémon Master is never ending, as we have been doing this for more than 25 years.

How many of these games have you played? You may be too young to have started back in the days of the Red and Blue versions, and despite some great remakes, you may have skipped a few of these games. If that is the case, I strongly suggest you find a way to play them all because they all contributed to the amazing franchise we have now.

I want to take this chance to talk about all of the main Pokémon games from nine different generations, and actually rank them just in case you feel like hopping into any of these. They are all really fun, but let us see which one catches your attention. Long-time players may not agree with this ranking, as it is purely the personal opinion of someone who has played every game at least twice.

10. Pokémon Black/White & Black 2/White 2 (Gen 5)

These games were arguably the least innovative Pokémon games so far. Yet, Game Freak felt so comfortable with Black & White that they even released direct sequels of the games to expand on the story happening just 2 years after what happened in Black & White. There were a total of 156 new Pokémon introduced this generation, and some of them are decent (like the starters Snivy, Tepig and Oshawott) but there were some really uninspired Pokemon as well like Patrat.

The story featured Team Plasma and the shady character simply called N, a bunch of forgettable characters, and even multiple rivals. All of these were signals of a story that begged to be forgotten in favor of some spotlight for the graphics and Pokémon battles themselves, which were not all that bad. But I have to admit that these games also aimed to be more mature and self-conscious, pondering on the idea of enslaving free creatures and storing them in tiny balls for the benefit of humanity. Quite an interesting idea - yes - but unfortunately it wasn't well written or developed throughout the games.

Between the first and second pair of games there were a ton of Legendaries too, and the concept of alternate forms was a bit exploited this time around. I am still not convinced we needed two Meloettas, Landorus, Thundurus, Tornadus and 3 different versions of Kyurem.

It may have not introduced a lot of technological features, but these were still pretty good games that were enjoyable and fun, and the concept of a direct sequel was attractive at the time. Despite being on the bottom of the list, these games are worthy of your time.

9. Pokémon Diamond/Pearl/Platinum (Gen 4)

These games represented quite a graphical leap forward for the Pokémon series in 2007. The Nintendo DS needed to show off its true potential, and these games did just that for the system. They were beautiful and made really good use of the innovative second screen on the system. These games were also the first to feature online trading and battling. And with 107 new Pokémon including the starters Turtwig, Chimchar and Piplup, this feature was a nice addition to complete the Pokédex easily.

The other big addition to the games was The Underground, a place meant to be played locally with others and an experience that I did not get to experiment with as much as I would have wanted. The Underground represented the very first time you could actually explore what was underneath the Hokkaido-inspired Sinnoh region in co-op. You could create secret bases and mine for valuable items in a pure and fun cooperative adventure.

Unfortunately, these technological leaps came along with a weak story filled with forgettable characters, Cynthia being the exception to this statement. I think the developers realized it was not such a great story, and that is why they also included beauty contests as a fun yet shallow secondary quest. The third game of this series; Platinum, added some cool features like alternate forms for Pokémon such as Shaymin and Rotom, and the very cool Distortion World.

Despite these flaws, the technological features here were enough to make these games memorable experiences for any Pokémon fan at the time. Plus, the online features of these games are the base of the current Pokémon experiences.

REMAKES:

Pokémon Brilliant Diamond /Shining Pearl

These were bound to be more modern than their older counterparts since they launched on the Nintendo Switch, so the transition was interesting, to say the least. The Underground from the classic games also evolved into The Grand Underground, which was actually a great end-game addition featuring different rare Pokémon to help you fill your Pokédex.

8. Pokémon X/Y (Gen 6)

These games were the first Pokémon adventures on the Nintendo 3DS and a true graphical advance compared to what we had before. Pokémon X/Y also changed the camera angle to accommodate this new perspective on the world and made great use of the system's second screen.

This generation only introduced 72 new Pokémon. Among these were the great starters Chespin, Fennekin and Froakie, as well as some new instant classics like Goodra and Sylveon. There was also a strong focus on Pokémon dual-types to balance the games nicely.

The main problem with these games was the story. It always seemed like these games just barely scratched the surface of the Pokémon mythology featured in the France-inspired Kalos region and focused instead on showing off the new looks and animations of these Pokémon games. The Legendaries and bad guys of these games were kind of uninspired. But these games featured one of the coolest mechanics in the franchise story: mega evolutions, which gifted us with great animations and some clutch moments in competitive play.

These games were also considered extremely easy thanks to this being the first time where Exp Share was not an optional thing. All of your Pokémon in your party gained Exp for each battle no matter what, and some players were not very happy with this design decision.

This was the first generation with no sequels nor third game that offered new mechanics, Pokémon or storyline. So many were left with a bit of curiosity for Zygarde and the potential of having a game more focused on this very interesting Pokémon.

7. Pokémon Sun/Moon (Gen 7)

This was probably the first time we noticed Game Freak wanted to shake things up a bit by eliminating the gym progression and introducing island trials, which involved tests and a battle with a powerful Pokémon. However, you still needed to fight an island's Kahuna afterwards, so you could say there was not a clear path ahead for Pokémon at this time.

On the bright side, the Hawaii-inspired region of Alola gifted us with 80 great new Pokémon including Rowlet, Litten and Popplio, which evolved into very cool Pokémon. Other fantastic additions included regional Alolan forms of old favorites like Exeggutor and Raichu. These games also expanded the Mega Evolution mechanic first introduced in the previous generation and experimented with a unique mechanic in the form of the very powerful and flashy Z-Moves.

The story was alright but predictable. These games suffer from some weak support characters like your rival, Hau. The Alola region also felt a bit disconnected due to its island design, but the 3DS delivered some really great graphics in both the overworld gameplay as well as Pokémon battles and animations.

These were strong entries in the series, but they were enhanced in the Ultra Sun and Ultra Moon "sequels" that launched just a year later with an alternate, yet very similar story. So these base versions aged to feel like non-essential games.

REMAKES:

Pokémon Ultra Sun/Ultra Moon

These games were weird to play. The story was pretty much the same, so playing an almost identical game all over again was a bit odd. However, we got a few new Ultra Beasts and a new form of Necrozma, both great additions to the competitive play. But the most important addition had to be Ultra Wormholes and the possibility of encountering Ultra Beasts in their own habitat.

6. Pokémon Sword/Shield (Gen 8)

These games represented the very first time Game Freak delivered a fully 3D Pokémon exploration experience on one of its most popular systems ever. These games delivered a great adventure featuring the Dynamax/Gigantamax phenomenon. The gym battles were transformed into fantastic sports-like matches, and battles really felt like something big and important.

The Galar region was beautiful to explore with some fantastic towns and sights. The map was based on the United Kingdom with the Wild Area serving as the main ground for exploration and wild Pokémon. Sword and Shield were the first games to introduce raid battles, offering new Pokémon periodically so the player base could keep playing for months after launch. This was a very good reason to connect to the internet and play with your friends to catch rare and even shiny Pokémon.

Grookey, Scorbunny and Sobble were not the most beloved starters, but their evolutions were amongst the most used Pokémon in competitive play during that generation.

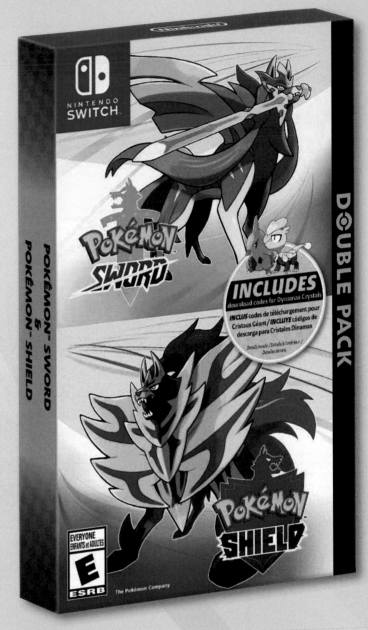

Sword and Shield were also the first games that featured a couple pieces of DLC (downloadable content). Both Isle of Armor and Crown Tundra introduced brand new areas to explore with beloved new Pokémon like Urshifu. There were even new Galarian regional variants like Slowpoke, Articuno, Zapdos and Moltres. A total of 89 Pokémon were introduced in this generation.

These games had a great reception among the press and users, and they were a great entry point for new fans of the series thanks to the fair difficulty and very attractive presentation on the Nintendo Switch.

5. Pokémon Scarlet/Violet (Gen 9)

Please refer to the Pokémon Scarlet & Violet review in this book for more details about these titles.

Scarlet and Violet were the titles that really applied new ideas introduced in Pokémon Legends: Arceus. This is the generation that finally delivered a fully realized 3D open world. There was more freedom of choice than ever, and multiple storylines that ended with a bang.

These games really felt new and exciting, and they featured some of the best Pokémon of the past decade, including the starters Spirigatito, Fuecoco and Quaxly. Complete online integration also meant more possibilities of PvP and PvE activities, and the possibility of DLCs could also breathe new life to these games for years to come.

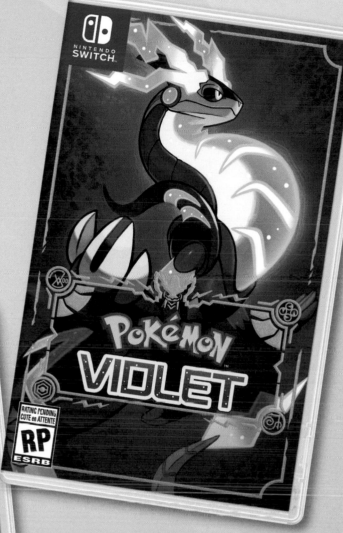

The truth is that we are deliberating on the true potential of these games. There have only been a few serious competitions as of this writing. We are getting more Pokémon via Tera Raid Battles and we are still experimenting with the potential of many new great Pokémon. But overall, the base games felt like an amazing, unique trip that only the Paldea region could provide. Characters are full of personality and it feels like they are only held back because of the lack of voice acting.

The only reason this generation is not higher on this list is because of the many heartbreaking bugs present in the games even months after launch and the technical flaws that are present in these games. But Scarlet and Violet brought us one of the best and most appealing Pokémon generations.

4. Pokémon Legends: Arceus (Gen 8)

I was hesitant about including this one but the truth is this game featured a new region, new Pokémon and some incredible new mechanics and innovations, so it is definitely one of the main Pokémon games in my book. Strictly talking though, it's a part of the 8th generation.

Pokémon Legends: Arceus was definitely a turning point in the series. What many called the "Breath of the Wild Pokémon" was not afraid to take more risks and change more stuff from the traditional formula than ever, and it truly felt like the best way to mess things up in the best possible way.

We are talking about an alternative way to fill the Pokédex, crafting mechanics, different battle styles and regional evolutions for beloved Pokémon such as the starters Rowlet, Cyndaquil and Oshawott. A total of 22 new Pokémon were featured here between new species and regional variants.

The game also featured a more serious story full of memorable characters and driven by Pokémon mythology. The fact that this game makes you a pioneer on Pokémon studies in a place where people and Pokémon were actually afraid of each other and live separately really hits different. The wide and vast regions of the Hisui region are an amazing exploration setting and you truly feel a freedom for exploration and progress that was a first in all Pokémon series.

Sadly, this game was held back by technical problems and poor visual quality. But those of us who were able to see past these setbacks had one of the most memorable titles in the series. It is quite a feat to finish the game and register the whole Pokédex as it is a fairly difficult game too! So, kudos if you were able to do and see everything this game has to offer.

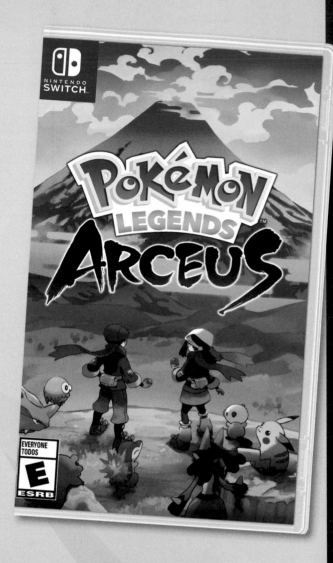

3. Pokémon Ruby/Sapphire/Emerald (Gen 3)

This was the generation that revolutionized the series with deeper mechanics such as natures, EVs and IVs. Now, it was not just about a specific Pokemon, but a properly natured and properly trained one. It really became a more complex game for those interested in the competitive side of Pokémon, and a much more satisfying game since your Pokémon truly felt unique and its power was a direct consequence of your decisions when training it.

Powered by the Game Boy Advance, this was also a generation of vibrant colors. Game Freak really did their best to make use of all the new capabilities of this portable console. We now had the chance to catch 135 different Pokémon, including the great starters Treecko, Torchic and Mudkip.

Hoenn was a great region to explore, big in size and diverse in biomes and Pokémon to catch. The Legendaries represented the power of nature, and we also got very creative Legendaries and event-only Pokémon such as Deoxys and Jirachi.

The Game Boy Advance was compatible with a special device that allowed you to read cards called the E-Reader, unlocking Pokédex entries and special mini games. These games were also compatible with the remakes of Pokémon Blue/Red and even Pokémon from the GameCube games to trade Pokémon. This means it was a time when all three generations melded nicely, and it was an amazing opportunity to pursue the task of completing a Pokédex in all these games.

REMAKES:

Pokémon Omega Ruby/Alpha Sapphire

Fans begged for Ruby and Sapphire remakes for years, and when they finally dropped, they did not disappoint. The 3DS was capable of breathing new life to this generation, and the developers even added some welcome changes to the formula. These games included competitive features such as Mega Evolution and Primal Reversion for Kyogre and Groudon.

2. Pokémon Red/Blue/Yellow (Gen 1)

I know ranking the older games on top of this list might seem like the result of pure nostalgia. But it still feels incredible to start a new save for these first Pokémon games. They are a true perfect trip down memory lane.

Of course, this is where it all started. The main 151 Pokémon we all know and love were here. I do not have to name the starters for you to instantly recognize them either. Plus, there was a great cast of characters that were very recognizable thanks to the anime: Team Rocket, Giovanni, Lance, etc. All the big names were here and served as the perfect vehicle to tell the original story we all know and love.

These are also the simplest games. The Yellow version enhanced everything about these games and allowed us to play out a story more similar to what was happening on the TV show. We were able to catch and train all of the starters too and, alongside Pikachu, live out the ultimate Kanto experience. If you were lucky enough, you also had a very special Pikachu Game Boy Color to match.

One great thing about these games was the vision the developers had to make two versions with some exclusive Pokémon you could only catch in one of them. Pokémon became a social thing, a weekend gathering for some battling and trading and a way for you to complete the Pokédex. You could only get Mew in special events, so owning one made you one of the cool kids in the neighborhood.

REMAKES:

Pokémon FireRed/LeafGreen

The very first remakes in Pokémon history came in 2004 with the FireRed and LeafGreen versions. These were beautiful remakes that represented a very nice trip down memory lane. Every part of the base games was beautifully remastered and the games felt familiar yet fresh and exciting. To be back in Professor Oak's lab choosing your very first Pokémon was a true gift for many of us.

1. Pokémon Gold/Silver (Gen 2)

Once the first generation of Pokémon became a hit, the second one was quite possibly the most expected and most exciting one. Back then leaks on the internet were really scarce. Magazines would talk about the development of the new fully-colored generation for the Gameboy Color console, and rumors were an everyday thing that lasted for months. I can remember Marill being leaked and even rumored to be catchable in Pokémon Yellow. We were crazy for some more Pokémon.

And then Gold & Silver dropped and it was AMAZING. It added 100 new Pokémon with all-time favorites like Scizor and Ampharos, as well as a great trio of starters (quite possibly my favorites).

This generation also made great use of an internal clock that made you care about day and night. Different Pokémon spawning at different times of the day was a brilliant idea that was well executed here. Besides the amazing Johto region, Kanto was also included! Seamlessly connected and available to tackle just as soon as you became the Johto champion. Here, you could face the 8 gym leaders from the original games and even face off against the champion of that region: Red. This gave an amazing sense of nostalgia that hit all the right notes even to this day.

Legendaries like Ho-Oh and Lugia were not only powerful but also really cool-looking, and the legendary trio of Raikou, Entei and Suicune were a pain to hunt thanks to them migrating through the map and constantly fleeing from you. These games also gifted us with the very first opportunity to find and hatch Pokémon eggs!

It is amazing how this all happened back in 1999. These are truly legendary Pokémon games and a must-play for any fan of the series.

REMAKES:

Pokémon HeartGold/SoulSilver

These were quite possibly the most requested remakes in the history of Pokémon. And the developers delivered a couple of great games that were equally respectful of the past and bold enough to push a few new ideas into the formula. This time you could have your lead Pokémon walk with you (a first since Pokémon Yellow!). A little extra nostalgia was added in the form of the Pokéwalker, a device that emulated the "Pokémon Pikachu" device, a Pokémon-themed Tamagotchi released back in 1998.

The Pokémon Pokédex

By Bill Gill

Thanks to 26 years of Nintendo video games, there are now over 1000 Pokémon in the Pokémon Universe. Satoshi Tajiri started working on his Pocket Monsters idea in 1989 and published his first Pokémon game in 1996. Most of his early Pokémon were based on bugs, plants, animals and mythological creatures. These basic ideas for Pokémon have grown tremendously over the last few of decades.

We thought it might be a nice reference for our readers to have a listing of every catchable Pokémon out there. Pokémon lists are usually broken into Generations. Each Generation represents a new title in the main RPG franchise. Most folks use Roman Numerals to represent each Generation.

Generation I
Red, Green, Blue and Yellow
151 NEW POKÉMON

Generation II
Gold, Silver and Crystal
100 NEW POKÉMON

Generation III
Ruby, Sapphire and Emerald
135 NEW POKÉMON

Generation IV
Diamond, Pearl and Platinum
107 NEW POKÉMON

Generation V
Black and White
156 NEW POKÉMON

Generation VI
X and Y
72 NEW POKÉMON

Generation VII
Sun and Moon, Ultra Sun and Ultra Moon, Let's Go, Pikachu! and Let's Go, Eevee!
88 NEW POKÉMON

Generation VIII
Sword and Shield, Legends: Arceus
96 NEW POKÉMON

Generation IX
Scarlet and Violet
103 NEW POKÉMON

As we write this book, there are 1008 Pokémon to catch out there!

Generation I

No.	Name						
001	Bulbasaur	039	Jigglypuff	077	Ponyta	115	Kangaskhan
002	Ivysaur	040	Wigglytuff	078	Rapidash	116	Horsea
003	Venusaur	041	Zubat	079	Slowpoke	117	Seadra
004	Charmander	042	Golbat	080	Slowbro	118	Goldeen
005	Charmeleon	043	Oddish	081	Magnemite	119	Seaking
006	Charizard	044	Gloom	082	Magneton	120	Staryu
007	Squirtle	045	Vileplume	083	Farfetch'd	121	Starmie
008	Wartortle	046	Paras	084	Doduo	122	Mr. Mime
009	Blastoise	047	Parasect	085	Dodrio	123	Scyther
010	Caterpie	048	Venonat	086	Seel	124	Jynx
011	Metapod	049	Venomoth	087	Dewgong	125	Electabuzz
012	Butterfree	050	Diglett	088	Grimer	126	Magmar
013	Weedle	051	Dugtrio	089	Muk	127	Pinsir
014	Kakuna	052	Meowth	090	Shellder	128	Tauros
015	Beedrill	053	Persian	091	Cloyster	129	Magikarp
016	Pidgey	054	Psyduck	092	Gastly	130	Gyarados
017	Pidgeotto	055	Golduck	093	Haunter	131	Lapras
018	Pidgeot	056	Mankey	094	Gengar	132	Ditto
019	Rattata	057	Primeape	095	Onix	133	Eevee
020	Raticate	058	Growlithe	096	Drowzee	134	Vaporeon
021	Spearow	059	Arcanine	097	Hypno	135	Jolteon
022	Fearow	060	Poliwag	098	Krabby	136	Flareon
023	Ekans	061	Poliwhirl	099	Kingler	137	Porygon
024	Arbok	062	Poliwrath	100	Voltorb	138	Omanyte
025	Pikachu	063	Abra	101	Electrode	139	Omastar
026	Raichu	064	Kadabra	102	Exeggcute	140	Kabuto
027	Sandshrew	065	Alakazam	103	Exeggutor	141	Kabutops
028	Sandslash	066	Machop	104	Cubone	142	Aerodactyl
029	Nidoran♀	067	Machoke	105	Marowak	143	Snorlax
030	Nidorina	068	Machamp	106	Hitmonlee	144	Articuno
031	Nidoqueen	069	Bellsprout	107	Hitmonchan	145	Zapdos
032	Nidoran♂	070	Weepinbell	108	Lickitung	146	Moltres
033	Nidorino	071	Victreebel	109	Koffing	147	Dratini
034	Nidoking	072	Tentacool	110	Weezing	148	Dragonair
035	Clefairy	073	Tentacruel	111	Rhyhorn	149	Dragonite
036	Clefable	074	Geodude	112	Rhydon	150	Mewtwo
037	Vulpix	075	Graveler	113	Chansey	151	Mew
038	Ninetales	076	Golem	114	Tangela		

Generation II

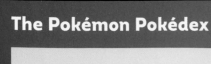

No.	Name						
152	Chikorita	177	Natu	202	Wobbuffet	227	Skarmory
153	Bayleef	178	Xatu	203	Girafarig	228	Houndour
154	Meganium	179	Mareep	204	Pineco	229	Houndoom
155	Cyndaquil	180	Flaaffy	205	Forretress	230	Kingdra
156	Quilava	181	Ampharos	206	Dunsparce	231	Phanpy
157	Typhlosion	182	Bellossom	207	Gligar	232	Donphan
158	Totodile	183	Marill	208	Steelix	233	Porygon2
159	Croconaw	184	Azumarill	209	Snubbull	234	Stantler
160	Feraligatr	185	Sudowoodo	210	Granbull	235	Smeargle
161	Sentret	186	Politoed	211	Qwilfish	236	Tyrogue
162	Furret	187	Hoppip	212	Scizor	237	Hitmontop
163	Hoothoot	188	Skiploom	213	Shuckle	238	Smoochum
164	Noctowl	189	Jumpluff	214	Heracross	239	Elekid
165	Ledyba	190	Aipom	215	Sneasel	240	Magby
166	Ledian	191	Sunkern	216	Teddiursa	241	Miltank
167	Spinarak	192	Sunflora	217	Ursaring	242	Blissey
168	Ariados	193	Yanma	218	Slugma	243	Raikou
169	Crobat	194	Wooper	219	Magcargo	244	Entei
170	Chinchou	195	Quagsire	220	Swinub	245	Suicune
171	Lanturn	196	Espeon	221	Piloswine	246	Larvitar
172	Pichu	197	Umbreon	222	Corsola	247	Pupitar
173	Cleffa	198	Murkrow	223	Remoraid	248	Tyranitar
174	Igglybuff	199	Slowking	224	Octillery	249	Lugia
175	Togepi	200	Misdreavus	225	Delibird	250	Ho-oh
176	Togetic	201	Unown	226	Mantine	251	Celebi

Generation III

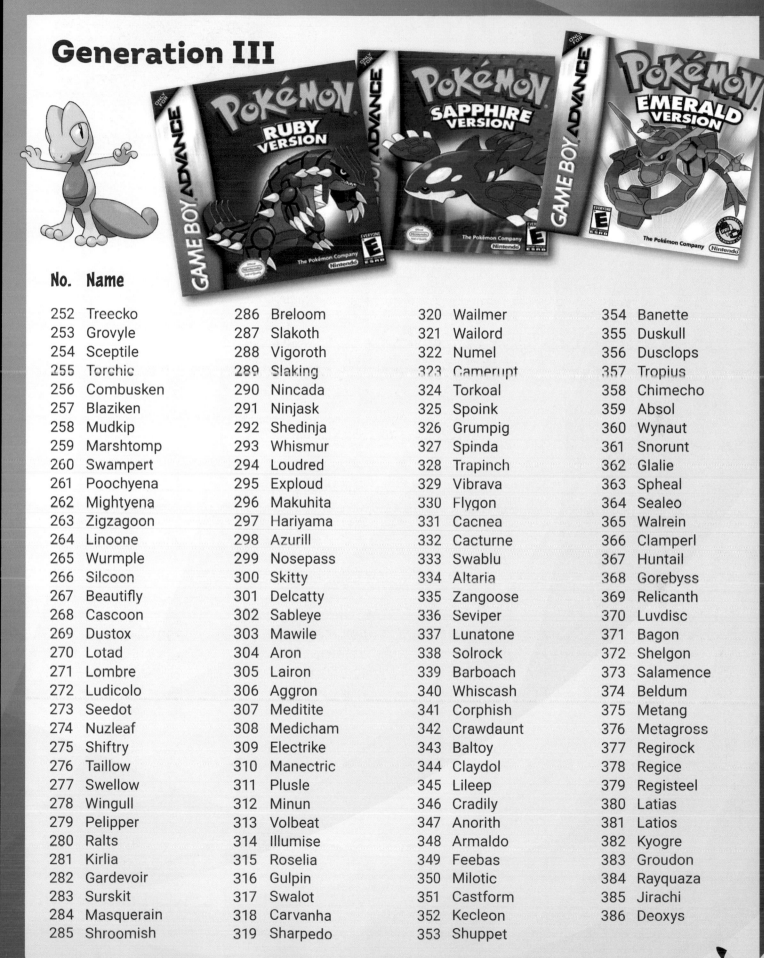

No.	Name	No.	Name	No.	Name	No.	Name
252	Treecko	286	Breloom	320	Wailmer	354	Banette
253	Grovyle	287	Slakoth	321	Wailord	355	Duskull
254	Sceptile	288	Vigoroth	322	Numel	356	Dusclops
255	Torchic	289	Slaking	323	Camerupt	357	Tropius
256	Combusken	290	Nincada	324	Torkoal	358	Chimecho
257	Blaziken	291	Ninjask	325	Spoink	359	Absol
258	Mudkip	292	Shedinja	326	Grumpig	360	Wynaut
259	Marshtomp	293	Whismur	327	Spinda	361	Snorunt
260	Swampert	294	Loudred	328	Trapinch	362	Glalie
261	Poochyena	295	Exploud	329	Vibrava	363	Spheal
262	Mightyena	296	Makuhita	330	Flygon	364	Sealeo
263	Zigzagoon	297	Hariyama	331	Cacnea	365	Walrein
264	Linoone	298	Azurill	332	Cacturne	366	Clamperl
265	Wurmple	299	Nosepass	333	Swablu	367	Huntail
266	Silcoon	300	Skitty	334	Altaria	368	Gorebyss
267	Beautifly	301	Delcatty	335	Zangoose	369	Relicanth
268	Cascoon	302	Sableye	336	Seviper	370	Luvdisc
269	Dustox	303	Mawile	337	Lunatone	371	Bagon
270	Lotad	304	Aron	338	Solrock	372	Shelgon
271	Lombre	305	Lairon	339	Barboach	373	Salamence
272	Ludicolo	306	Aggron	340	Whiscash	374	Beldum
273	Seedot	307	Meditite	341	Corphish	375	Metang
274	Nuzleaf	308	Medicham	342	Crawdaunt	376	Metagross
275	Shiftry	309	Electrike	343	Baltoy	377	Regirock
276	Taillow	310	Manectric	344	Claydol	378	Regice
277	Swellow	311	Plusle	345	Lileep	379	Registeel
278	Wingull	312	Minun	346	Cradily	380	Latias
279	Pelipper	313	Volbeat	347	Anorith	381	Latios
280	Ralts	314	Illumise	348	Armaldo	382	Kyogre
281	Kirlia	315	Roselia	349	Feebas	383	Groudon
282	Gardevoir	316	Gulpin	350	Milotic	384	Rayquaza
283	Surskit	317	Swalot	351	Castform	385	Jirachi
284	Masquerain	318	Carvanha	352	Kecleon	386	Deoxys
285	Shroomish	319	Sharpedo	353	Shuppet		

Generation IV

No.	Name

No.	Name	No.	Name	No.	Name	No.	Name
387	Turtwig	414	Mothim	441	Chatot	468	Togekiss
388	Grotle	415	Combee	442	Spiritomb	469	Yanmega
389	Torterra	416	Vespiquen	443	Gible	470	Leafeon
390	Chimchar	417	Pachirisu	444	Gabite	471	Glaceon
391	Monferno	418	Buizel	445	Garchomp	472	Gliscor
392	Infernape	419	Floatzel	446	Munchlax	473	Mamoswine
393	Piplup	420	Cherubi	447	Riolu	474	Porygon-Z
394	Prinplup	421	Cherrim	448	Lucario	475	Gallade
395	Empoleon	422	Shellos	449	Hippopotas	476	Probopass
396	Starly	423	Gastrodon	450	Hippowdon	477	Dusknoir
397	Staravia	424	Ambipom	451	Skorupi	478	Froslass
398	Staraptor	425	Drifloon	452	Drapion	479	Rotom
399	Bidoof	426	Drifblim	453	Croagunk	480	Uxie
400	Bibarel	427	Buneary	454	Toxicroak	481	Mesprit
401	Kricketot	428	Lopunny	455	Carnivine	482	Azelf
402	Kricketune	429	Mismagius	456	Finneon	483	Dialga
403	Shinx	430	Honchkrow	457	Lumineon	484	Palkia
404	Luxio	431	Glameow	458	Mantyke	485	Heatran
405	Luxray	432	Purugly	459	Snover	486	Regigigas
406	Budew	433	Chingling	460	Abomasnow	487	Giratina
407	Roserade	434	Stunky	461	Weavile	488	Cresselia
408	Cranidos	435	Skuntank	462	Magnezone	489	Phione
409	Rampardos	436	Bronzor	463	Lickilicky	490	Manaphy
410	Shieldon	437	Bronzong	464	Rhyperior	491	Darkrai
411	Bastiodon	438	Bonsly	465	Tangrowth	492	Shaymin
412	Burmy	439	Mime Jr.	466	Electivire	493	Arceus
413	Wormadam	440	Happiny	467	Magmortar		

Generation V

No. Name

No.	Name	No.	Name	No.	Name	No.	Name
494	Victini	533	Gurdurr	572	Minccino	611	Fraxure
495	Snivy	534	Conkeldurr	573	Cinccino	612	Haxorus
496	Servine	535	Tympole	574	Gothita	613	Cubchoo
497	Serperior	536	Palpitoad	575	Gothorita	614	Beartic
498	Tepig	537	Seismitoad	576	Gothitelle	615	Cryogonal
499	Pignite	538	Throh	577	Solosis	616	Shelmet
500	Emboar	539	Sawk	578	Duosion	617	Accelgor
501	Oshawott	540	Sewaddle	579	Reuniclus	618	Stunfisk
502	Dewott	541	Swadloon	580	Ducklett	619	Mienfoo
503	Samurott	542	Leavanny	581	Swanna	620	Mienshao
504	Patrat	543	Venipede	582	Vanillite	621	Druddigon
505	Watchog	544	Whirlipede	583	Vanillish	622	Golett
506	Lillipup	545	Scolipede	584	Vanilluxe	623	Golurk
507	Herdier	546	Cottonee	585	Deerling	624	Pawniard
508	Stoutland	547	Whimsicott	586	Sawsbuck	625	Bisharp
509	Purrloin	548	Petilil	587	Emolga	626	Bouffalant
510	Liepard	549	Lilligant	588	Karrablast	627	Rufflet
511	Pansage	550	Basculin	589	Escavalier	628	Braviary
512	Simisage	551	Sandile	590	Foongus	629	Vullaby
513	Pansear	552	Krokorok	591	Amoonguss	630	Mandibuzz
514	Simisear	553	Krookodile	592	Frillish	631	Heatmor
515	Panpour	554	Darumaka	593	Jellicent	632	Durant
516	Simipour	555	Darmanitan	594	Alomomola	633	Deino
517	Munna	556	Maractus	595	Joltik	634	Zweilous
518	Musharna	557	Dwebble	596	Galvantula	635	Hydreigon
519	Pidove	558	Crustle	597	Ferroseed	636	Larvesta
520	Tranquill	559	Scraggy	598	Ferrothorn	637	Volcarona
521	Unfezant	560	Scrafty	599	Klink	638	Cobalion
522	Blitzle	561	Sigilyph	600	Klang	639	Terrakion
523	Zebstrika	562	Yamask	601	Klinklang	640	Virizion
524	Roggenrola	563	Cofagrigus	602	Tynamo	641	Tornadus
525	Boldore	564	Tirtouga	603	Eelektrik	642	Thundurus
526	Gigalith	565	Carracosta	604	Eelektross	643	Reshiram
527	Woobat	566	Archen	605	Elgyem	644	Zekrom
528	Swoobat	567	Archeops	606	Beheeyem	645	Landorus
529	Drilbur	568	Trubbish	607	Litwick	646	Kyurem
530	Excadrill	569	Garbodor	608	Lampent	647	Keldeo
531	Audino	570	Zorua	609	Chandelure	648	Meloetta
532	Timburr	571	Zoroark	610	Axew	649	Genesect

Generation VI

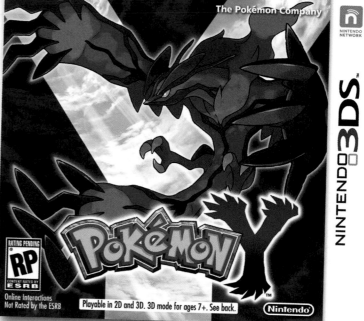

No. Name

No.	Name	No.	Name	No.	Name	No.	Name
650	Chespin	668	Pyroar	686	Inkay	704	Goomy
651	Quilladin	669	Flabébé	687	Malamar	705	Sliggoo
652	Chesnaught	670	Floette	688	Binacle	706	Goodra
653	Fennekin	671	Florges	689	Barbaracle	707	Klefki
654	Braixen	672	Skiddo	690	Skrelp	708	Phantump
655	Delphox	673	Gogoat	691	Dragalge	709	Trevenant
656	Froakie	674	Pancham	692	Clauncher	710	Pumpkaboo
657	Frogadier	675	Pangoro	693	Clawitzer	711	Gourgeist
658	Greninja	676	Furfrou	694	Helioptile	712	Bergmite
659	Bunnelby	677	Espurr	695	Heliolisk	713	Avalugg
660	Diggersby	678	Meowstic	696	Tyrunt	714	Noibat
661	Fletchling	679	Honedge	697	Tyrantrum	715	Noivern
662	Fletchinder	680	Doublade	698	Amaura	716	Xerneas
663	Talonflame	681	Aegislash	699	Aurorus	717	Yveltal
664	Scatterbug	682	Spritzee	700	Sylveon	718	Zygarde
665	Spewpa	683	Aromatisse	701	Hawlucha	719	Diancie
666	Vivillon	684	Swirlix	702	Dedenne	720	Hoopa
667	Litleo	685	Slurpuff	703	Carbink	721	Volcanion

Generation VII

No.	Name	No.	Name	No.	Name	No.	Name
722	Rowlet	744	Rockruff	766	Passimian	788	Tapu Fini
723	Dartrix	745	Lycanroc	767	Wimpod	789	Cosmog
724	Decidueye	746	Wishiwashi	768	Golisopod	790	Cosmoem
725	Litten	747	Mareanie	769	Sandygast	791	Solgaleo
726	Torracat	748	Toxapex	770	Palossand	792	Lunala
727	Incineroar	749	Mudbray	771	Pyukumuku	793	Nihilego
728	Popplio	750	Mudsdale	772	Type: Null	794	Buzzwole
729	Brionne	751	Dewpider	773	Silvally	795	Pheromosa
730	Primarina	752	Araquanid	774	Minior	796	Xurkitree
731	Pikipek	753	Fomantis	775	Komala	797	Celesteela
732	Trumbeak	754	Lurantis	776	Turtonator	798	Kartana
733	Toucannon	755	Morelull	777	Togedemaru	799	Guzzlord
734	Yungoos	756	Shiinotic	778	Mimikyu	800	Necrozma
735	Gumshoos	757	Salandit	779	Bruxish	801	Magearna
736	Grubbin	758	Salazzle	780	Drampa	802	Marshadow
737	Charjabug	759	Stufful	781	Dhelmise	803	Poipole
738	Vikavolt	760	Bewear	782	Jangmo-o	804	Naganadel
739	Crabrawler	761	Bounsweet	783	Hakamo-o	805	Stakataka
740	Crabominable	762	Steenee	784	Kommo-o	806	Blacephalon
741	Oricorio	763	Tsareena	785	Tapu Koko	807	Zeraora
742	Cutiefly	764	Comfey	786	Tapu Lele	808	Meltan
743	Ribombee	765	Oranguru	787	Tapu Bulu	809	Melmetal

Generation VIII

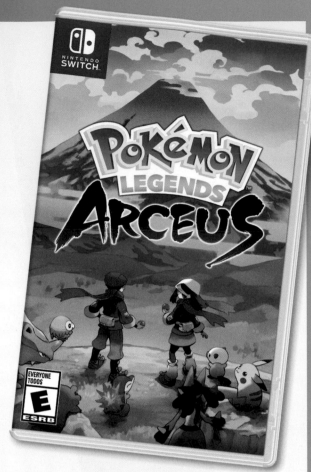

No. Name

No.	Name	No.	Name	No.	Name	No.	Name
810	Grookey	834	Drednaw	858	Hatterene	882	Dracovish
811	Thwackey	835	Yamper	859	Impidimp	883	Arctovish
812	Rillaboom	836	Boltund	860	Morgrem	884	Duraludon
813	Scorbunny	837	Rolycoly	861	Grimmsnarl	885	Dreepy
814	Raboot	838	Carkol	862	Obstagoon	886	Drakloak
815	Cinderace	839	Coalossal	863	Perrserker	887	Dragapult
816	Sobble	840	Applin	864	Cursola	888	Zacian
817	Drizzile	841	Flapple	865	Sirfetch'd	889	Zamazenta
818	Inteleon	842	Appletun	866	Mr. Rime	890	Eternatus
819	Skwovet	843	Silicobra	867	Runerigus	891	Kubfu
820	Greedent	844	Sandaconda	868	Milcery	892	Urshifu
821	Rookidee	845	Cramorant	869	Alcremie	893	Zarude
822	Corvisquire	846	Arrokuda	870	Falinks	894	Regieleki
823	Corviknight	847	Barraskewda	871	Pincurchin	895	Regidrago
824	Blipbug	848	Toxel	872	Snom	896	Glastrier
825	Dottler	849	Toxtricity	873	Frosmoth	897	Spectrier
826	Orbeetle	850	Sizzlipede	874	Stonjourner	898	Calyrex
827	Nickit	851	Centiskorch	875	Eiscue	899	Wyrdeer
828	Thievul	852	Clobbopus	876	Indeedee	900	Kleavor
829	Gossifleur	853	Grapploct	877	Morpeko	901	Ursaluna
830	Eldegoss	854	Sinistea	878	Cufant	902	Basculegion
831	Wooloo	855	Polteageist	879	Copperajah	903	Sneasler
832	Dubwool	856	Hatenna	880	Dracozolt	904	Overqwil
833	Chewtle	857	Hattrem	881	Arctozolt	905	Enamorus

Generation IX

No.	Name

No.	Name	No.	Name	No.	Name	No.	Name
906	Sprigatito	932	Nacli	958	Tinkatuff	984	Great Tusk
907	Floragato	933	Naclstack	959	Tinkaton	985	Scream Tail
908	Meowscarada	934	Garganacl	960	Wiglett	986	Brute Bonnet
909	Fuecoco	935	Charcadet	961	Wugtrio	987	Flutter Mane
910	Crocalor	936	Armarouge	962	Bombirdier	988	Slither Wing
911	Skeledirge	937	Ceruledge	963	Finizen	989	Sandy Shocks
912	Quaxly	938	Tadbulb	964	Palafin	990	Iron Treads
913	Quaxwell	939	Bellibolt	965	Varoom	991	Iron Bundle
914	Quaquaval	940	Wattrel	966	Revavroom	992	Iron Hands
915	Lechonk	941	Kilowattrel	967	Cyclizar	993	Iron Jugulis
916	Oinkologne	942	Maschiff	968	Orthworm	994	Iron Moth
917	Tarountula	943	Mabosstiff	969	Glimmet	995	Iron Thorns
918	Spidops	944	Shroodle	970	Glimmora	996	Frigibax
919	Nymble	945	Grafaiai	971	Greavard	997	Arctibax
920	Lokix	946	Bramblin	972	Houndstone	998	Baxcalibur
921	Pawmi	947	Brambleghast	973	Flamigo	999	Gimmighoul
922	Pawmo	948	Toedscool	974	Cetoddle	1000	Gholdengo
923	Pawmot	949	Toedscruel	975	Cetitan	1001	Wo-Chien
924	Tandemaus	950	Klawf	976	Veluza	1002	Chien-Pao
925	Maushold	951	Capsakid	977	Dondozo	1003	Ting-Lu
926	Fidough	952	Scovillain	978	Tatsugiri	1004	Chi-Yu
927	Dachsbun	953	Rellor	979	Annihilape	1005	Roaring Moon
928	Smoliv	954	Rabsca	980	Clodsire	1006	Iron Valiant
929	Dolliv	955	Flittle	981	Farigiraf	1007	Koraidon
930	Arboliva	956	Espathra	982	Dudunsparce	1008	Miraidon
931	Squawkabilly	957	Tinkatink	983	Kingambit		

Rare Pokémon Finds

Japanese Pocket Monsters Video Intro Set - 1999

This Video Intro Set was designed to teach kids how to play the Pokémon Trading Card Game. This Intro Set included:

- A VHS Instructional Video Cassette
- 2 Small Decks (40 cards each)
- 1 Playmat (paper)
- 1 Rulebook
- 1 Bag of Damage Counters
- 2 Poison Status Markers
- 1 Custom Coin

What we love most about this set are the cool Pokémon cards you find inside. The cards are a mix of Base Set cards through Neo cards. The cards in the Squirtle deck have Squirtle symbols, and the cards in the Bulbasaur deck have Bulbasaur symbols. The standouts are the holographic Venusaur and the holographic Blastoise. None of these cards have rarity symbols on them, which is unusual, making these cards a little more valuable than their counterparts.

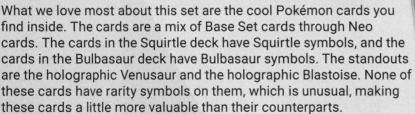

Poké Card Creator Pack - 2004

In 2004, the Kids' WB! Television Network had a Pokémon art contest for kids aged 5 to 15. The Grand Prize Winners had their art displayed on this special set of Pokémon cards. There are only five cards in the set, and all five cards are in this Creator Pack. About 5,000 packs were printed of this special set. These packs were awarded as prizes to the winners and random contest entrants.

JR East Pokémon Stamp Rally - 1997

During the summer of 1997, Pocket Monsters and Japan Railways (JR) launched the first Pokémon Stamp Rally. Kids were invited to ride the train and collect Pokémon stamps from 30 different train stations along the route. As a final reward for collecting all 30 stamps, participants would receive a special folder containing Surfing Pikachu and Mew. These two cards are affectionately called "Mt. Fuji Pikachu" and "Lilypad Mew". These Pokémon Stamp Train Rallies still continue in the Japan, and the prizes have changed over the years.

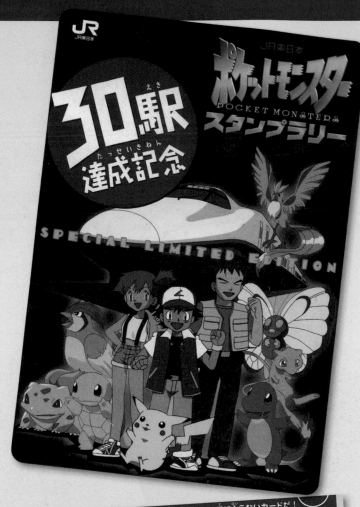

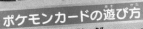

ポケモンカードの遊び方

知ってる人はおさらいしよう、知らない人は覚えよう。ポケモンカードは楽しさいっぱいのカードゲームだ！！

1 プレイヤーはお互いに、カード60枚を組み合わせた山（デッキと呼びます）を持ち寄ります。

2 お互いに自分の「デッキ」から対戦ポケモンカードを出し合って、ポケモンの「ワザ」で戦います。

3 自分のポケモンにエネルギーカードをつけて、「ワザ」が使えるようになるまで育てます。

4 ポケモンは、より強力に進化させることができます。

5 「トレーナーカード」をつかってポケモンたちの戦いを手助けすることができます。

6 先に相手のポケモンを6匹倒した方が「勝ち」です。

ポケモンカードシリーズ

ポケモンファンなら見逃せない、楽しいアイテムが大集合！

スターターパック
（価格1300円・税抜き）

ポケモンカードを始めるために必要な基本のデッキ（60枚セット）だ。エネルギーカードはこのスターターパックにしか入っていないぞ。種類1種は負けない。また、カードは200種以上にもなるので、友だちとのトレーディング（交換）で完全コレクションを目指すのも楽しいぞ！

カウンターセット
（価格400円・税抜き）
ダメージカウンター＆毒マーカーのセット。ゲームを盛り上げるぞ！

拡張パック
ポケモンジャングル
化石の秘密
（価格291円・税抜き）
カード10枚入り。これらを購入してコレクションをもっと増やそう。

公式カードファイル
（価格500円・税抜き）
104枚もカードをファイルできる。おまけカードも1枚入っているぞ！

プレイマット
裏・陽・表
（価格1300円・税抜き）
NBAのコートをイメージしたゲーム専用のマットだ。おまけカード1枚付く！

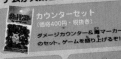

★アニメの主題歌がCDになった！ポケモンカードCMソング「ポケモン言えるかな？」も入って950円（税別）で発売中。

©1995,1999 NINTENDO/CREATURES/GAME FREAK ●制作／クリーチャーズ ●発売元／メディアファクトリー

発売されているカードには入っていないぞ！ここでしか手に入らないカードだ！

なみのりピカチュウ LV.13　HP50

ねずみポケモン；身長0.4m、体重6kg

●● なみのり　30

ある夏休み、波の高い海岸で、なみのりをしているピカチュウが見られた。

— にげる

● 弱点

No.025

Mini Technical Atoli

なみのりピカチュウ の特徴

名前
「なみのりピカチュウ」はいままでの「ピカチュウ」とは名前が違う。つまり、夢の8枚入りピカチュウデッキが可能になるのだ！

イラスト
当然、初公開のオリジナル版だ！！やっぱりピカチュウはかわいいね。

ワザ
「なみのり」のワザは少ない消費エネルギーで、相手にダメージを与えることができる。

ミュウ の特徴

幻のポケモン
151匹目のポケモンとして謎に包まれている「ミュウ」。カードゲームでも「ミュウ」は貴重な存在だ。

特殊能力
ミュウは進化ポケモンからのワザを受けないぞ。敵が進化して強くなったときに登場させよう！

ワザ
ねんりきの力は弱いが、コインを投げて相手をマヒさせることができる！少しずつ相手を追いつめよう！！

ミュウ　LV.8　HP40

しんしゃポケモン；身長0.4m、体重4.0kg

[特殊能力] ニュートラルシールド

● ねんりき　10
コインを投げて「おもて」なら、相手を「マヒ」状態にする。

— にげる

● 弱点

制作：ゲームフリーク・クリーチャーズ／協力：メディアファクトリー

ANA Pokémon Airlines Promos – 1997, 1998

Did you know there are real Pokémon Airplanes flying around the world? There have been more than 15 different Pokémon jets flying the friendly skies. The early jets were all owned by All Nippon Airways (ANA). The first Pokémon jet (1998) was a Boeing 747, and if you flew on it, you would get a Flying Pikachu card and a Dragonite card. The second Pokémon jet (1998) was a Boeing 767, and when you flew on it, you would earn a different Flying Pikachu card and an Articuno card.

Those two jets are now retired, but there are still 6 Pokémon jets flying amongst the clouds. The newest Pokémon jet is owned by China Airlines, and is an Airbus 321. Wouldn't you love to go for a ride on one?

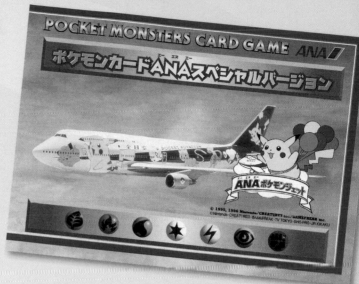

Pokémon Box – Ruby & Sapphire (GameCube) – 2004

The Pokémon Box was a Pokémon utility for Pokémon players. You could only buy this at the Pokémon Center in New York City. The Pokémon Box included:

- 1 Nintendo GameCube GameBoy Advance Cable
- 1 Nintendo GameCube Memory Card
- 1 Pokémon Box Ruby & Sapphire GameCube Disc

Trainers could store up to 1,500 Pokémon from Ruby & Sapphire with this package. The setup also allowed players to play Ruby & Sapphire on their TVs, which was extremely cool at the time. After Pokémon were stored, players could look through all the stats of each Pokémon on the television. The Pokémon Box eventually let trainers store captured Pokémon from Emerald, FireRed and LeafGreen as well.

This bundle is extremely rare to find in complete condition - with all components and the original packaging. Many owners threw away the outside cardboard box that held all the contents. Complete copies can sell for several thousand dollars.

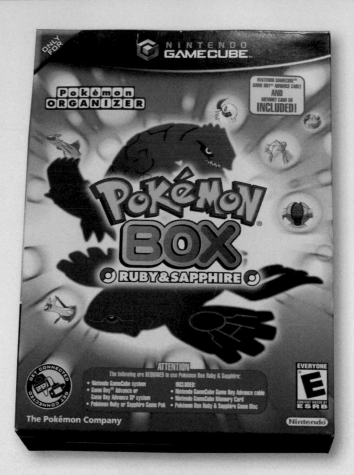

Game Boy Color – 3rd Anniversary Pokémon Center Edition – 1999

This was a beautiful Limited Edition Game Boy Color that you could only buy at the Pokémon Center in Tokyo in 1999. The screen frame features Charmander, Squirtle, Bulbasaur, and Pikachu. The shell of the system is orange and blue. The red power indicator is in Charmander's tail! We also love those Pikachu batteries that came with it!

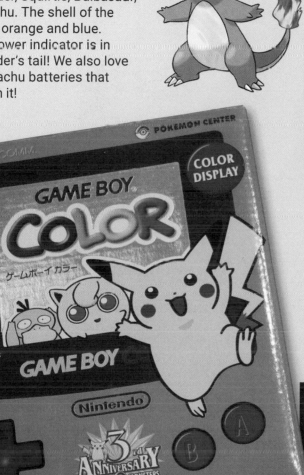

Puzzles

Ash's Strongest Pokémon Word Search

Find and circle each of the words from the list below.
Words may appear forwards or backwards, horizontally, vertically or diagonally in the grid.

```
S E T I N O G A R D A K U K O R C H I F
B B M I L P Q O A O A O G E E O C O P M
E M E L M E T A L Z R R M I F C S K X V
L R H E K I N G L E R K D C Q S M E W S
I U G I Y O I R A C U L Q O H I X E D T
T H N S S O R C A R E H D R O L E I N A
P C N O J X A D S O U U V N N G E L J R
E A O T I M A I R L A N I A U N P A K A
C K R E O V S L N A R B I C R S A L R P
S I K L R X E I R C C A A Y A U N G O T
H P J W S O N R R O I O G L E C R C O O
H A W O H F X A N F N N V N H N E I K R
C H A R I Z A R D Z E S E I E Y F S O V
M I A J N I N E R G I T R R S G N J D E
A R R E T R O T M J A T C Y O H I Y I Y
E M U H Y F F E T T T B V H N A E L L L
T P T W S W E L L O W E D O D U R U E Q
```

Melmetal Greninja Noivern Lycanroc Staraptor Sirfetchd Infernape
Gengar Goodra Swellow Torterra Snorlax Pikachu Sceptile
Dracovish Incineroar Krookodile Dragonite Heracross Charizard
Kingler Gliscor Lucario Rowlet Glalie

Pokémon Scarlet & Violet Word Search

Find and circle each of the words from the list below. Words may appear forwards or backwards, horizontally, vertically or diagonally in the grid.

```
Y W L P Y S P E G Z I P I I C R N D P E
X E Q J L O I I C E N S T B D S P A A H
D E U V R E H O U N D S T O N E R G E T
O C A T T P G T O E D S C R U E L M U K
N U X F D I C R Z G T D C I D P N T G F
D C L K U U B X I I H E E E E I G K O O
O N Y I O E P M N D A O E R F F U P R T
Z C O A D U C K A D E B L A C S Q H A I
O E F D I Y A O A G A L L D I A C H M T
V R I E I T O R C X N A E U E Y R F R A
E U L M O A A V C O P I T K O N D R A G
R L F N L C R A D O X S K S S P G W F I
O E P U S T L O R W L I Z A E N E O H R
Q D D W I I A W K F A R I G I R A F A P
K G O F B A N N I H I L A P E M F A T S
S E I U M A B O S S T I F F U E M O C U
M R R G A R G A N A C L M I R A I D O N
```

Quaxly   Skeledirge   Garganacl   Ceruledge   Annihilape   Baxcalibur
Gholdengo   Meowscarada   Houndstone   Armarogue   Toedscruel
Kingambit   Sprigatito   Mabosstiff   Dondozo   Fuecoco   Koraidon
Tinkaton   Miraidon   Farigiraf   Palafin

Ash's Traveling Companions

Over the last 25 years, Ash has made quite a few friends. How well do you know Ash's pals? Here is a Crossword Puzzle with 16 of Ash's closest traveling companions. After each clue, in parentheses, is a hint with a Pokémon that friend has. The answer key is at: pojo.com/cw-ash

Across

4. Clemont's younger sister (Clemont's Dedenne)
5. Daughter of Professor Cerise (Yamper)
6. Gym Leader of the Lumiose City Gym (Luxray)
11. A strong trainer from Opelucid City (Axew)
13. Dreams of becoming Akala Island's kahuna (Charizard)
14. A Pokémon Coordinator from Petalburg City (Blaziken)
15. May's younger brother, and a Pokémon Trainer (Jirachi)
16. A Pokémon Performer from Vaniville Town (Sylveon)

Down

1. She wears her father's Z-Ring on her wrist (Alolan Vulpix)
2. Pokémon Coordinator from Twinleaf Town (Piplup)
3. His goal is to catch Mew (Cinderace)
4. Gym Leader of Pewter City Gym (Onix)
7. She wears a green Z-Ring given to her by an Oranguru (Bounsweet)
8. A Pokemon Watcher (Marill)
9. A Pokémon Connoisseur from Striaton City (Pansage)
10. A water-type Pokémon specialist classmate of Ash's (Popplio)
12. Hapu gave him a Z-Ring as reward (Togedemaru)
15. Gym Leader of Cerulean City Gym (Starmie)

Pokémon Alphabet Challenge

For every letter of the alphabet, can you come up with a Pokemon name starting with that letter?

A _____

B _____

C _____

D _____

E _____

F _____

G _____

H _____

I _____

J _____

K _____

L _____

M _____

N _____

O _____

P _____

Q _____

R _____

S _____

T _____

U _____

V _____

W _____

X _____

Y _____

Z _____

TRIVIA

As of Generation IX, there are 134 Pokémon whose names begin with "S", making it the most frequently used initial letter. The least frequently used initial letter is "X" with only 3 names starting with the letter "X".

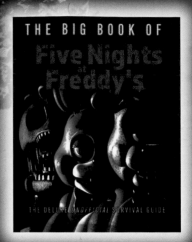